ROYAL GARDENERS

ROYAL GARDENERS

The History of Britain's Royal Gardens

ALAN TITCHMARSH

BBC BOOKS

CONTENTS

INTRODUCTION

*V*isit any royal palace or stately home today, and there is a sense that the solid architecture, mature gardens and surrounding natural landscape have remained unchanged for centuries.

But history isn't like that. If you sell your own home, you know that the new owners are going to knock it about a bit, however hard you worked to make it perfect. It's exactly the same with royal palaces – only more so. Countless generations of owners will have altered, added and, in many cases, knocked down and started again from scratch. And when it comes to the garden, the chances are that it will have seen even more make-overs as fashions and requirements changed.

Houses and land were the 'currency' of royalty and the aristocracy, and the more rich and powerful the family, the more residences, farms and glamorous gardens they owned. Royalty, not surprisingly, needed to outshine everyone else.

Royal homes and gardens would be passed down through the generations, and also bought, sold, leased, swapped, given away as gifts or used as bribes whenever the need arose. So one way and another, the house and garden you see today is the product of centuries of change.

The royals were the trend-setters of their day, simply because they had the money and the motivation to innovate. What royalty did first, rich aristocratic families copied, so new styles, 'star' gardeners and must-have plants percolated down through society. Eventually, a watered-down version would work its way slowly down the social scale to the lower orders, whose gardens trailed behind the fashions by several generations.

But for gardening to flourish, it took three key ingredients – peace, prosperity and a reigning monarch (or more likely his wife) who was keen on garden-making. Since British history is packed with rulers whose fingers were far from green, I've exercised editorial control and ruthlessly weeded out of this book any king or queen whose reign didn't make a significant contribution to gardening history.

I've divided them up chronologically, and for those of us who left school a long time ago, I've included a full list of kings and queens whose reigns fall within each chapter so you can see where the gardening monarchs fit in the running order.

And if you always hated history at school, take comfort from the fact that wars and politics don't get a look-in (except when they directly impinge on gardening), and dates are kept to a bare minimum, so read on in complete confidence.

But if you are expecting nothing but regal hearts and flowers, gentle romance and pastoral idylls, be warned – royal garden history is packed with intrigue, skulduggery and dirty doings.

OPPOSITE: The history of Britain's royal gardeners is as colourful as the gardens they created.

1066 AND ALL THAT

The trouble with gardens is that they don't 'keep'. Over 1,000 years, owners tend to lose interest and let them go, or else successive generations make so many alterations that nothing is left of the original scheme – which is why no medieval gardens still exist in their original form.

All the information we have to show what they once looked like comes from old tapestries and illuminated manuscripts, where a certain amount of artistic licence may well have come into play. Household accounts and building contracts, preserved in family archives, sometimes show details of spending on gardens. Early poetry and literature, such as *The Romance of the Rose* and some of Chaucer's stories, often describe gardens and the plants that grew in them, but they were written in romantic terms rather than giving the sort of factual information that a gardener would find useful.

Rare early gardening books are valuable for building up a picture of the plants that were available at various times, but dates of plant introductions were very often not recorded at the time. The best garden historians can do nowadays is trace them back to the earliest known reference in a book – which explains why 'job lots' of plant-introduction dates coincide with the dates of major herbals and other important books.

What are not very reliable are the stories that were passed by word of mouth, as they often experienced a good deal of alteration or misunderstanding before being written down. This is why we have so many conflicting stories over 'garden myths and mysteries', such as who really introduced the potato.

But one thing we do know is that, in the autumn of 1066, William, Duke of Normandy, arrived on Pevensey beach with a 12,000-strong army and became William I of England (alias William the Conqueror) after his success in the battle of Hastings. The Normans had landed.

WILLIAM THE CONQUEROR'S CASTLES

Now, it's all very well taking over a turbulent country – which England was then – but it's quite another to hang on to it, and that's where the Normans' talent for castle-building paid dividends. William put up castles all around the country, particularly at large towns such as Lincoln, Colchester, Cambridge, Norwich, Guildford, Exeter and York, where a show of strength was needed to quell the locals.

But most of his castles weren't made of stone, since they took specialist craftsmen several years to build. They were 'instant' castles made of earth and timber, which could be quickly slung together by unskilled labour. They were a typical Norman design known as motte and bailey castles. The 'motte' was a mound of earth on which stood a wooden tower or 'keep', and the 'bailey' was a courtyard surrounded by a ditch next to a tall fence, which acted as a first line of defence against intruders. It was very effective. If your bailey was overrun by attackers, you simply shinned up your motte, locked yourself in the tower and rained arrows down on the milling hordes below.

OPPOSITE ABOVE: The gardening bug bit even in medieval England, and castle courtyards gave way to basic ornamental gardens and spaces for contemplation.
OPPOSITE BELOW: Prebendel Manor, in Northamptonshire, is a stunning example of a reconstructed medieval garden.

BELOW: *Medieval gardens were often enclosed within castle walls, where food was grown for the owner and family.*

OPPOSITE: *The parkland at Windsor Castle was originally used by William the Conqueror as his own personal hunting ground.*

William's men brought their very first castle across the Channel with them in self-assembly form – the first-ever flat-pack – in order to make a safe 'base' at Hastings straight after the battle. Only when the country was reasonably under control were the wooden castles gradually replaced by stone ones.

The Normans shipped some of their building stone over from Caen in France, but they also took over the stone quarries in England to supply castle-building materials. A typical stone Norman castle had much the same design as the earlier earth and wooden one it replaced. There'd be a four-storey keep, divided up inside into rooms for the castle owner and his family (lined with tapestries to keep the draughts out), and storerooms filled with provisions so that the castle could withstand a siege. The servants and other hangers-on lived in wooden huts built up against the inside of the stone walls surrounding the castle.

And here's where our story really starts, because in the centre of this area was an open courtyard which would later evolve into a very basic ornamental garden.

Windsor Sets a Trend

Of all the castles built by William the Conqueror, only one can claim 1,000 years of continuous royal occupancy: Windsor Castle. Built in 1070 as part of the outer ring of fortifications that the Normans constructed around London, it was deliberately perched on the only high ground for miles, which made the castle easy to defend.

Although the site was chosen for sound strategic reasons, the big attraction for William was the nearby forest, which had been a popular Saxon hunting ground. Hunting was his favourite sport, so the accommodation was improved and Windsor became one of his hunting lodges. It wasn't until around the year 1100 that a later king, Henry I, bought the land immediately around the castle and made a garden.

The original Norman castle and its early garden have long since been swallowed up by generations of extensions, improvements and alterations by successive monarchs.

To impress the people of London, who were not easily conquered, William ordered the construction of his grandest castle of all – the Tower of London. This was a four-storey square tower, which was built from stone right from the start and whitewashed to make it stand out. Since the King and his court regularly stayed there, it was fitted out with much better living quarters than the average castle of its time. Later kings added outer defences, extra living accommodation and gardens, and it was to be a royal residence for some time before turning into a top people's prison and execution centre. Nowadays it's more light grey than white, and houses the Crown Jewels.

Royal Hunting Parks

It was William the Conqueror who first introduced the Norman sport of deer-hunting to England, and he set up a series of royal hunting parks especially for that purpose.

In Hampshire he created what is now the New Forest, evicting local peasants from the land and planting trees to make a better habitat for deer. At the time the word 'forest' didn't have quite the same meaning as today: a forest was a place for hunting – the trees were quite incidental.

It was in the New Forest that William the Conqueror's successor, Rufus the Red, met his end after receiving an arrow in his eye while out hunting. It was fired by Walter Tyrell, and historians still wonder whether it was an accident or murder. The place is commemorated by the Rufus Stone, thoughtfully signposted off the A31 near Cadnam, just west of Southampton.

The *Domesday Book*, compiled in 1086 to list the nation's assets, shows that around 25 royal hunting forests had been established throughout the realm. It's been reckoned that they occupied almost one-third of all the land in the country.

Henry I, William the Conqueror's youngest son, created what was arguably the first 'royal' garden when, in 1123, he enclosed a chunk of land at Woodstock in Oxfordshire (which much later became Blenheim Palace) and turned it into a royal hunting park. Not content with the usual deer, he walled off one enclosure to make a menagerie, which he stocked with exotic animals including lions, leopards, lynx, camels and what is reputed to have been a solitary porcupine, sent as a gift from a relative in Montpellier.

The royal hunting parks were maintained exclusively for royalty and nobility. Only the blue-blooded could shoot deer and wild boar; lesser noblemen were allowed to shoot lower-class game, but woe betide the local peasant who fancied a rabbit for dinner. Penalties were draconian: you could be blinded or have a hand cut off – or worse. Times were tough for the hungry peasantry, while William himself struggled with a weight problem.

EARLY EDIBLE GARDENS

Throughout medieval times, decorative gardens were a luxury known only to royalty and the most powerful noblemen, who lived in substantial, well-fortified homes. Monasteries, which were also immensely wealthy, had well-developed gardens mainly for 'useful' plants. Even in medieval times there was a gigantic 'swap' system operating between religious establishments throughout Europe. At the bottom end of the social scale, the poor were self-sufficient peasants who lived off the land and didn't have the time for decorative gardening, even if they had the inclination.

ABOVE: To help him settle into England William introduced some Norman pastimes, most notably deer-hunting, which started the tradition of royal hunting parks.

OPPOSITE: The White Tower at the Tower of London was built in the eleventh century as a royal residence. Many guests were entertained there – before it became a prison.

ABOVE LEFT: *Henry II invested a lot of money in creating gardens for his royal palaces and is most famous for creating a garden for his wife at Winchester, and a bower for his mistress, Rosamund, at Woodstock.*

ABOVE RIGHT: Rosa gallica *'Versicolor' started life as* Rosa mundi – *named after Henry II's mistress, the Fair Rosamund.*

OPPOSITE: *Queen Eleanor's garden in Winchester has recently been restored and is now a beautiful and historically accurate medieval castle garden.*

Monastery Gardens

A medieval monastery was much more than a retreat from the world. Monks educated the children of the aristocracy, for whom Latin and French (thanks to Norman rule) were compulsory. Monks practised medicine and, since there were no printed books, they also copied and illustrated manuscripts by hand.

A monastery was a self-sufficient community. Within the grounds were productive gardens for growing fruit, nuts and vegetables, based on the agricultural estates the Romans had established 1,000 years earlier. Since monks were restricted in eating meat, and the Benedictine orders were not allowed meat at all, monasteries also had fish ponds where they kept carp for the pot. These were known, rather unappetizingly, as stew-ponds.

The monastery had its own infirmary, plus a pharmacy where herbal remedies were prepared and a garden for medicinal plants. The garden was arranged with almost military precision, each variety of plant being grown in its own individual square bed. These were arranged in a chessboard pattern, divided by sand or gravel paths, so that plants could be conveniently gathered in all weathers. Since they don't seem to have used labels, medical monks had to know their plants – and it's thought that they grew as many as 400–500 species. But these were purely medicinal, and would not have been grown in 'pleasure gardens'.

Decorative gardens hardly figured in monasteries. There was a central quadrangle of grass surrounded by a cloistered walk, where the monks could circulate for exercise when it rained. At bigger establishments the abbot would have a private garden for meditation, and there might also be a cemetery – for abbots only.

THE FIRST ROYAL GARDENS UNDER HENRY II AND ELEANOR OF AQUITAINE

Henry II continued the castle-building tradition and he seems to have taken an interest in proper gardens, encouraged by his French wife, Eleanor of Aquitaine. Eleanor was a well-travelled lady, who had been to the Holy Land with her first husband, Louis VII of France, and so would have seen Islamic gardens, as well as Moorish copies in southern Europe. The Arabs ruled Spain from 711 to the time of Columbus, in 1492, and their enclosed formal gardens were familiar to the Normans, who had themselves ruled part of Spain for a while. As a result, the Islamic influence was to have an effect on English royal garden style for many centuries.

Since the royal court needed to travel around the country regularly, gardens started to appear at all the stopping-off points on the regal rounds. Under Henry II, gardens began to blossom at Woodstock and at Winchester, which was then the capital city. Henry also made gardens at York and at Arundel Castle.

At Woodstock Henry II continued improving the grounds that Henry I had originally used as his park, and not purely for aesthetic reasons. He'd married Eleanor for her money, and he soon took a mistress – Rosamund Clifford, the Fair Rosamund, after whom *Rosa mundi* (*Rosa gallica* 'Versicolor') was named. Their meeting place was a bower that he built at Everswell, in the grounds at Woodstock.

Don't go thinking of a rustic garden seat with roses growing on an arch over the top – no, this was a far more regal version, comprising a trio of cottages with a natural spring-fed water garden nearby. All that remains now is the site, but at the time it started

Lawn maintenance

Compared to a modern lawn, a medieval flowery mead was relatively self-sufficient. Here's what passed for routine lawn care at the time.

BELOW: Flowery meads were all the rage in medieval times, not unlike our modern trend for wild-flower lawns.

Cutting: Grass was cut two or three times a year. Progress was slow: three men with scythes could cut an acre of grass in a day. The grass was then swept up with besom brooms and was usually fed to animals. Grass continued to be cut with scythes until the invention of the lawnmower in 1830.

Edging: Lawn edges were trimmed with a sickle. It would be almost impossible to do this around a modern lawn with conventional 'gully' edges, but the raised flowerbeds of a medieval garden made the job very much easier.

Feeding: Grass was never fed. Low levels of nutrients, especially nitrogen, prevented it from growing vigorously, but are ideal for the wild flowers, periwinkle and herbs that grew in medieval turf, which don't like heavy feeding. Call it cultivation by omission, but it worked.

Raking: Rakes were used to gather up moss, which would have been a big problem in medieval turf because of poor surface drainage. This was partly caused by the construction method. Turf was beaten down well when it was laid, to make a smooth, level surface – essential, as it would have been impossible to cut a bumpy lawn with scythes. But, being small, lawns would also have been very heavily trampled as people traversed them regularly in all weathers, which wouldn't have helped the moss problem either.

a trend, and a rash of romantic 'Rosamund's bowers' appeared in upper-crust gardens all round the country. Not surprisingly, Eleanor wasn't thrilled when she found out what was going on, so she arranged for Rosamund's murder. Allegedly.

One of the most important of Henry II's royal residences was Winchester Castle. He and Eleanor spent a great deal of time at Winchester which, besides being the capital city, was close to the south-coast port of Southampton with its convenient sailings for Normandy – handy when they needed to cross the water to see relatives and generally fly the flag. So to make the place more homely, they had a garden made at Winchester Castle in 1178.

Although the original medieval garden has not survived, if you visit Winchester today you can see Queen Eleanor's Garden, behind the Great Hall, looking almost exactly as it would have done at the time. Re-created comparatively recently after extensive research, it is reckoned to be the most historically accurate medieval castle garden around, featuring trelliswork 'cloisters' planted with vines, surrounding a square of 'flowery mead' with a seat and raised beds for scented plants, such as roses, edged with wattle.

ABOVE: Gardens in the Middle Ages were places for quiet reflection and often included seats surrounded by scented plants.

OPPOSITE: *The re-created medieval garden at Prebendal Manor has been designed to illustrate the elements of a fourteenth-century garden. It includes ornamental gardens as well as sections for self-sufficiency, medicinal herbs and privacy and contemplation.*

In fact, not one but three Queen Eleanors contributed to the original garden, in quick succession; the wives of Henry II, Henry III and Edward I were all Eleanors – of Aquitaine, Provence and Castile respectively.

GARDENING THE MEDIEVAL WAY

Castle gardens in medieval times were 'gardens of pleasure' enclosed well inside the walls, where the ladies of the court could stroll, sit and gossip, or simply amuse themselves reading or playing chess safely away from the riff-raff. The gardens were pleasantly perfumed but small – space would have been at a premium.

Lawns as such didn't exist, but in their place was a flowery mead which was halfway between a lawn and a walk-through flowerbed, where grass was studded with a huge mixture of wild flowers. There were turf seats, like wooden benches filled with soil and topped with turf planted with fragrant herbs, such as chamomile and thyme. Similar seats were sometimes made round large trees, using a wall of woven sticks to hold the soil in place round the trunk, with a layer of turf laid on top.

Arbours were popular, too, but they were usually simple structures of wooden poles, or woven osier (willow) 'trellis' supporting honeysuckle or grapevines. Tunnel arbours – a long row of arches over a path – would be planted with bindweed (*Calystegia silvatica*), the white one with flowers like church bells that today we revile as a weed. While we

rave about the non-invasive blue version called morning glory, the Normans were less picky and knew a robust plant when they saw it.

Decorative wells or springs would often have been the centrepiece of the garden, though at grander establishments there would sometimes have been more elaborate water features such as pools and fountains, based on ideas 'borrowed' from Moorish gardens.

Flowerbeds were laid out formally – a chessboard pattern was very popular. Each bed was raised slightly with woven osier panels, something like today's miniature sheep hurdles, to keep the soil off the paths. Paths were made of sand or gravel to provide a well-drained, all-weather surface. Plants

were mixed together to make a floral 'tapestry' that looked good and perfumed the air – highly necessary at a time when everyday life was distinctly pungent, and plumbing was still at the 'bucket and chuck it' stage.

MEDIEVAL SELF-SUFFICIENCY

Wealthy landowners with big estates lived on meat – especially game – plus fruit and vegetables grown in their own grounds and bread from their farms. All kinds of exotic items such as dates, citruses, pomegranates and dried fruit were imported from abroad, though the cost was enormous and only royalty and very wealthy noble families could afford them.

Market gardens of a sort existed from medieval times onwards around big cities, supplying fresh food for people without big gardens of their own. This produce was sold at street markets. Out in the countryside, peasants lived mainly on potage – a sludge of dried peas, and oats or other cereals stewed up in a big pot over the living-room fire and flavoured with potherbs – vegetables or culinary herbs that they grew or picked in the wild. Even a spot of poaching was still off-limits.

Not surprisingly, the most important plants for medieval people were ones that they could eat, though the range was fairly unexciting. Before the Normans arrived, food plants were largely limited to what already grew wild in England, such as wild cabbage, seakale and leeks, plus any survivors of the fruit and vegetables the Romans had brought with them, such

Warden pie

To make Warden pie, boil pears in wine (any modern variety will do), grind in a pestle and mortar (or blender) then heat with some honey, ginger and cinnamon. When cool, thicken with egg yolks. (Adding saffron gives the yellow colouring characteristic of medieval food.) Pour into a pastry case (or coffin, as they were alarmingly known) and cook again.

BELOW: Although ornamental gardens were fashionable, self-sufficiency was an important element in medieval gardens.

as figs and lettuces. Norman introductions, and odds and ends brought back by knights returning from the Crusades, increased the range available but it still seems rather basic to us today.

Apples were either 'pearmains' (a general term for a type of apple rather than the name of a variety), 'costards' (a particularly large apple, sold by costermongers) or cider apples. Warden pears were cultivated by Cistercian monks at Warden Abbey, Bedfordshire, and remained the popular variety for several centuries. They were a large baking variety, traditionally used to make Warden pies. The fruit took a very long time to ripen, and stayed rock hard for months after picking – 'good keepers' as catalogues would describe them nowadays. Storage facilities were not very sophisticated, so fruit that 'kept' through the winter was a lot more desirable then than it is nowadays. Nuts were also much grown, for the same reason.

Herbs were widely grown, not just for cooking but for a huge range of other uses. Since there were no high street shops, a medieval housewife had to make everything she needed to run the family home from basic ingredients – plants. They were used for scenting linen, to deter fleas, for strewing on the floor to kill smells and soak up spills (they were swept up and replaced regularly), for first aid, dyeing wool and flavouring ale or wine. The 'herbs' were mostly English native wild flowers, plus a fairly small list of imported species. Many of their common names today still reflect their original uses – think of bedstraw, eyebright, self-heal, woundwort and fleabane.

THE EMERGENCE OF DECORATIVE GARDENS

Henry III's marriage to Eleanor of Provence in 1236 brought herds of her French relatives to court, and with them came a taste for luxurious living and garden-making that quickly percolated throughout the medieval court.

With Eleanor's encouragement, Henry spent a fortune on the gardens at the royal residences, which by now included Windsor, the Tower of London, Westminster, the manor of Guildford, Nottingham Castle, Gloucester Castle, the manor of Kempton in Middlesex, Arundel Castle, Marlborough Castle and Clarendon – his palatial hunting lodge near Salisbury, set in the biggest deer park in the country.

At Winchester Castle, Henry built the Great Hall and added three herbers (small enclosed flower gardens). But his biggest project was at Woodstock, where he built proper gardens for the first time in its history. In 1249 he had a small garden constructed, and a year later he had it enclosed with walls to make a herber 'in which the Queen may disport herself'. Two years later he had the garden turfed, and subsequently added another two herbers. He had a large new pool surrounded by a great cloister made at Everswell (the site of Rosamund's bower) and had a bench built and some decorative iron trelliswork put up.

Henry III's reign marked the end of the time that royal gardens were run by pen-pushers: from now on master gardeners would be appointed.

William the Gardener, who worked on the King's London gardens, was paid 3d (about 1p) per day. At the same time, at Windsor, Emo the Gardener was paid 2d a day.

Top gardeners at major gardens often got perks as well as their wages – free robes, grace and favour accommodation, and sometimes 'all the apples left on the trees when they are shaken'.

A PAUCITY OF PLANTS?

Today's gardener is spoilt for choice. We can grow any of the 90,000 or so plants that are available at garden centres and, in smaller numbers, from specialist nurseries all around. Things were very different in medieval times.

In the twelfth century the Abbot of Cirencester, Alexander Neckham, knew of 200 plants, including flowers, vegetables and agricultural crops. We know this because he mentions them in his book *De Naturis Rerum* (Of Natural Things), written around 1190, and also in a very long poem in which a couple of verses are devoted to plants. However, Abbot Neckham's list includes a number of species that were probably not grown in England, which he'd have met on trips abroad or encountered thanks to his foster-brother Richard I (the Lionheart), who must have brought back souvenirs from the Crusades – chickpeas, ebony, olives, nutmeg, date palms and pomegranates. I say they *probably* weren't grown in England because the climate was going through a long and unusually mild spell, which meant that vines and vineyards thrived, and all sorts of tenderish novelties might have grown in the south. But, discounting foreign oddities and purely medicinal plants, the total number of decorative garden species was likely to have been roughly 100 in about 1400.

By Henry VIII's reign, a century later, the total was still only 200. It wasn't till Elizabethan times and the start of serious long-distance exploration that new plants began to arrive in huge numbers, but organized plant-hunting expeditions didn't come about until much later. The grand days of plant-hunters and plant-hunting didn't start till the eighteenth century.

ABOVE: One of the earliest plant-hunters, Richard the Lionheart probably brought exotic souvenirs back from the Crusades, introducing new plants to medieval England.

THE EVOLUTION OF GARDEN TOOLS

Medieval gardeners used the same basic tools that we'd recognize today, which have changed very little since the Stone Age. More sophisticated materials and special-purpose gadgets have been added to the list only comparatively recently.

Primitive tools

Around 40,000 years ago Neolithic man used a primitive mattock, made from a sharp horn tied to a stick, for digging, or a 'digging stick', a sort of glorified dibber made from a mammoth's rib. When he needed a shovel, he used the shoulder blade of an ox. Like the bone in your Sunday roast lamb, it's a natural trowel, but a lot bigger.

BELOW: Tools at Prebendal show that medieval gardeners had similar ideas to us.

Mattocks are still used in places such as Africa, where the tool is lifted over the shoulder and brought down hard like a pickaxe. It is a good, robust tool for breaking up solid ground.

A 'digging stick', on the other hand, is sunk vertically into the soil and used with a lever action. By the time it had evolved into a primitive spade, a bar was sometimes added so that you could press down with your foot to push the thin blade into the soil without bruising your instep. Spades are best for dealing with relatively soft soil, particularly ground that's been regularly cultivated.

Over many centuries the mattock has fallen out of favour as a digging tool, but in my part of Hampshire – where it is known as a 'beck' – it is still the best thing to use for digging up tree stumps and tackling overgrown ground.

Medieval tools

Only a limited range of basic gardening tools was available in medieval England, and each one was a direct descendant of an agricultural implement.

An inventory taken at Abingdon Abbey in 1389 lists spades, shovels, rakes, trowels, scythes, sickles, baskets, sieves, ladders, axes, saws and shears – and that would have been a pretty good collection.

For general digging, mattocks and spades were both still in common use. Mattocks were the rough end of the market – wooden handles with heavy-duty metal heads. Spades were either made entirely of wood, or they'd be reinforced with a metal 'horseshoe' round the tip of a half-moon-shaped wooden blade. Superior models had a complete metal sheath wrapped round a square wooden blade. Medieval spades came in a big variety of shapes and sizes, which were all used for different jobs, and they looked rather irregular as they were mostly home-made.

Scythes were used for cutting grass, which would then be cleared up with a wooden, agricultural-style hayrake, and the sickle – a smaller version of the type used for agriculture – was used for trimming round the edges and for cutting hedges. Billhooks were used for most cutting jobs around the garden, including trimming shrubs. Draw-hoes with long blades were used for weeding. For watering people used the same terracotta jugs that were used in the house for fetching domestic water supplies. Around the 1500s the jugs 'grew' short, stumpy terracotta spouts with perforated 'roses',

ABOVE: Tunnel arbours provided important areas of shade to protect the pale complexions of medieval women as they took their daily stroll.

but it took centuries for them to lose their jug shape and start to look like modern watering cans.

Woven hazel, willow or chestnut baskets were used for general fetching and carrying; the first 'wilbarewe' (wheelbarrow) appeared in medieval times, though it looked more like a handcart on which you stood baskets of plants, or weeds or rubbish.

Much later ...

Writer and gardening pioneer John Evelyn described 70 tools in 1659. Proper cutting tools didn't start to appear much until the sixteenth century, when fruit trees and formal clipped plants became fashionable. The first garden shears were the same as the tools used for cutting hair and for shearing sheep. The high hedges of the seventeenth century were cut with a tool that looked like a long-handled sickle. Secateurs and hedge-clippers didn't appear until the nineteenth century.

But as gardening became more sophisticated, all sorts of weird and wonderful gadgets appeared, reaching a peak in Victorian times when there were tools for jobs that, nowadays, you'd never think of doing – like straightening your cucumbers.

Until quite late in history, garden tools were handmade. On large estates there would be a resident blacksmith and carpenter, but elsewhere you'd rely on the village smith.

OPPOSITE: *Gardens of the wealthy often had areas for the family to relax and enjoy the fragrance of herbs and other scented plants – which served the double purpose of masking the odours of medieval sewage systems! This re-created medieval garden at Prebendal has been planted in this style.*

OPPOSITE: *The Alhambra (pictured) and Generalife gardens in Granada, southern Spain, are classic examples of Islamic style, incorporating water features and courtyards.*

A good read

One of the first gardening books written in English – Latin being the language of scholars until late medieval times – was written by John Gardener in the fourteenth century. He lists just 97 plants. John Gardener was actually John the Gardener, who worked for the king at Windsor; like a lot of early surnames, John's came from what he did for a living.

Gardens for the Royal Roadshow

From the medieval period onwards, royal gardens were steadily improved, altered and extended, but they weren't the only ones. The nobility were at it, too.

Successive kings and their courts had to travel around the country dispensing law and order on the hoof. The king's own residences were not always convenient, so it became the custom for the royal party to be 'put up' by well-heeled aristocrats with castles or extensive fortified manor houses of their own.

As the size of the royal roadshow increased, generous hosts ultimately needed to be capable of accommodating a house party of up to 300 people – all eating heartily, and needing entertainment to take their minds off the primitive sanitation. As rivalry for the king's favour grew, a productive garden with sporting and leisure facilities became essential for rich and powerful noble families as a way of currying favour. And as times became more prosperous and peaceful, more extensive gardens developed outside castles and grand manor houses.

Herbers were placed adjacent to the house, usually under the windows of the owners' bed-chamber, and those of 'special' guests, where people could look down on them and appreciate the scent. Further away from the building would be a 'pleasaunce', a sort of decorative orchard planted with ornamental species as well as fruit trees, but still enclosed by secondary walls as security from casual thieves and brigands (there were a lot of them about). The pleasaunce was more than just a productive area. It was also used for entertaining guests, singing and dancing, playing chess and for games – sometimes even jousting tournaments.

Grand gardens might also have a gloriet (from the Spanish word for a small square) – a cross between a decorative grandstand and a summer-house – it was an essential ingredient of a Moorish garden.

THE LEGACY OF ELEANOR OF CASTILE

The Moorish influence on garden layout increased under Edward I thanks to his Spanish wife, Eleanor of Castile. From her marriage dowry Eleanor bought Leeds Castle, the remains of an old Norman ruin which stood on three rocky 'islands' in boggy land in north Kent. Edward built a new castle on the biggest of these, and on the second Eleanor built a cloistered courtyard garden with a gloriet in the middle, reached by a bridge. The two were surrounded by a deep moat made by damming the river Len. On the third island Edward built a barbican to defend the dam.

Queen Eleanor is credited with having introduced the concept of bathing to England, and after her death left some money to have a bathhouse built at the castle. Before bathrooms were invented, the upper classes (the only ones who bothered) took a bath in a portable tub. In winter this would be stood in front of the fire in the bedchamber, but in summer it was put outside under a tall, decorative tent of the sort used by crusaders, which had standing room. Illustrations of the time also show people bathing in water features around the grounds – a carry-over from early Islamic gardens.

Eleanor of Castile was an incredibly keen gardener; in 1279 she took over the lease of King's Langley in Hertfordshire and made her own garden, bringing gardeners over from Aragon, a melting pot

of cultures, which produced what were considered to be the elite horticulturists of Europe.

After Edward returned from the Crusades, however, the couple concentrated their gardening power on the Tower of London and the Palace of Westminster, where they planted roses and fruit. Quince trees were grown so that Eleanor could enjoy a traditional Spanish dish – quince marmalade.

Gardening was going through a miniboom: market gardens were thriving, fruit trees and vegetable seeds were being traded by specialist merchants, royal gardens were being upgraded, and gardens of the nobility by now often featured 'king's gardens' specially for the use of royalty on their travels around the country. But it was not to last for long. Shortly after Edward died there was a massive economic downturn that kept gardening in the doldrums until Tudor times.

The Islamic Influence

Islamic gardens as promised to the faithful are described in the Q'ran, which were copied as earthly representations. This style was also inspired by the earlier gardens invading Muslims encountered in Persia. Called *pairadaeza*, these multipurpose hunting park-cum-orchard-cum-pleasure gardens dated back to around 900BC.

Since Islamic gardens symbolize paradise on earth, it's not surprising to find that the design is full of religious overtones. The typical garden is a formal, square or rectangular courtyard enclosed by high walls, with two canals that cross to divide the garden into four plots representing the four quarters of the universe. In the centre of the garden it's traditional to have a water feature or a pavilion, and the area is planted with scented flowers and fruiting trees.

Moorish gardens

Islamic garden style was very practical for hot, dry countries. Water was a valuable resource and a dust-free humid space must have seemed like paradise. In hot countries today gardens are still built at the heart of the house. The rooms surround a courtyard with a water feature that acts as natural 'air-conditioning'.

RANUNCULUS ASIATICUS *fior pleno rubro* | *Rannuncolo di giardino*

A sticky end

Robin Hood fans will be glad to know that it was a plant that got King John in the end. He died in 1216 after over-indulging in peaches and new cider: it seems the peaches were green, causing a fatal attack of the collywobbles. In more ways than one, King John got his just desserts.

In the Middle East these would have been date palms or pomegranates, but as they didn't grow well in most of Europe other fruit trees were used there.

The essential ingredients of an Islamic garden paradise were shade, water and an abundance of fresh food, but illustrations usually also show a lot of very attractive young ladies, often larking about in various stages of undress in the water features – hence the high walls.

Enter the Moors

Following their conquest of Spain, the Arabs ruled there from 711 to 1492, and Moorish gardens became popular. Despite the slow pace of travel in medieval times, a surprising amount of long-distance travel went on as royal courts moved around, visiting relatives in Europe and keeping tabs on their overseas landholdings and properties, so new ideas travelled too – and royals were just the people to start new crazes back home. Foreign wives, like Eleanor of Castile, introduced familiar features from their homelands to spice up their new gardens and stop themselves feeling homesick.

Contributions from the Crusades

Among the big people-movers of medieval times were the Crusades. Several waves of knights set out with armies to recover Christian religious sites from the Muslims; the first Crusade to capture the Holy Land from the Turks was in 1096–9, and the second followed in 1147. Richard the Lionheart spent most of his reign crusading, which led to a lot of trouble with his next of kin – not least, King John.

The gardening upshot of the Crusades was that several new plants were brought back from Turkey and the Near East. These included the turban buttercup (*Ranunculus asiaticus*) and the hyacinth (*Hyacinthus orientalis*, not the large florist's hyacinths we know today, which weren't developed until much later). Another welcome outcome was that crusaders saw Islamic gardens, which inspired the basic square-grid pattern that was to become the standard layout for noble medieval gardens.

Conversion to Christianity

Naturally, the religious establishments back at home in England made a bit of a fuss about the use of non-Christian symbols in 'our' gardens, but they conveniently re-arranged the facts to suit themselves – and not for the first time. Christmas was an old pagan tradition that had been 'cleaned up' to suit the Christian Church.

The crossing canals of Islamic gardens became Christ's cross, and the garden now represented the Garden of Eden described in the Book of Genesis instead of the Islamic idea of paradise. The Church also 'bent' the stories behind plants to suit itself: the pure white Madonna lily was seen to symbolize the purity of the Virgin Mary, and roses with their

Medieval Plants

These rank as some of the most popular plants grown in medieval gardens when a relatively limited choice was available.

Edibles

Alexander – yellow-flowered member of the cow parsley family (*Smyrnium olusatrum*), which now grows wild in hedgerows, flowering in late spring; buds, young leaves and roots were used as salad, potherbs and root vegetables.

Colewort – wild cabbage; non-hearting plants used as loose leaves.

Corn salad – small, fast-growing salad plant, newly fashionable for winter salads.

Good King Henry (*Chenopodium bonus-henricus*) – perennial used as a green vegetable.

Orache (*Atriplex hortensis*) – native hardy annual used as salad plant or potherb, and eaten as a 'tonic' in spring.

Parsley

Turnip

Radish

Fennel

Saffron (*Crocus sativus*) – grown for flavouring, as a food colour and as a fabric dye.

Chives

Southernwood

Coriander

Sage

Savory

Hyssop

Mint – native British plant.

Rue

Dittany or dittander – a wild cousin of horseradish, whose root was used in a similar way; the hot-tasting leaves were also used for salad.

Smallage – wild 'leaf' celery, used as a salad leaf or potherb; you can still buy seeds today from specialist seed firms.

Lettuce

Costmary

Garden cress – the cress out of mustard and cress.

Onion

Leek

Garlic

Peas – not green peas at this stage; these were the sort for drying for winter potages, and were probably grown in fields along with cereal crops.

Medieval householders also used a lot of wild plants we'd call weeds nowadays as salad and potherbs.

Currants, red, white and black – all British natives, but in unimproved form.

Gooseberry – again, unimproved British native species.

Wild strawberry

Wild raspberry

Apples

Pears

Bullaces

Wild cherry

Grapevine

Medlars – probably only in the south of England.

Hazel

Chestnut

Walnut – known as 'great nut'.

Flowers and shrubs

Roses – *Rosa eglanteria*, the sweet briar with apple-scented leaves; *Rosa gallica* 'Versicolor' (*Rosa mundi*); *Rosa gallica* var. *officinalis* (the Apothecary's rose, the Red Rose of Lancaster); *Rosa alba* (the White Rose of York); *Rosa centifolia* (Cabbage rose).

Madonna lily (*Lilium candidum*)

Wild pansy, heartsease

Heliotrope – which was called 'turnsole' in medieval times.

Orpine (*Sedum telephium*) – a succulent wild flower that looks something like a pale, leggy version of *Sedum spectabile*.

Periwinkle

Hepatica – known rather misleadingly as liverwort.

Helleborus foetidus

Wallflower

Honeysuckle, wild (*Lonicera periclymnum*) – British native.

Mandrake (*Mandragora officinarum*) – the mystical medicinal plant, the man-shaped roots of which were said to scream when pulled out of the ground. A dog had to be tied to the plant to do the job as the puller would be driven mad.

Violet

Poppy (*Papaver rhoeas*)

Daffodil – native wild species.

Peony (*Paeonia officinalis*)

Cowslip

Foxglove

Gentian

Primrose

Daisy

Iris

Hollyhock

Lavender

Pinks (*Dianthus plumarius* and *D. caryophyllus*) – the parents of garden pinks, used for mulled wines and ales.

Hawthorn (*Crataegus monogyna*) – British native.

Elder (*Sambucus nigra*) – British native.

Privet (*Ligustrum vulgare*) – British native; this has narrow leaves and often sheds them in cold winters, unlike the oval-leafed privet introduced from Japan in the 1800s, which became the popular Victorian suburban hedging plant.

LEFT: The Norman Gateway, or Tower, was actually built in the reign of Edward III, c. 1359. The chambers above the archway were used as prison cells – James I of Scotland found himself there between 1413 and 1424.

prickles and blood-red flowers represented the crown of thorns and blood of Christ.

The more sensational sensual elements of the Islamic paradise gardens weren't at first glance catered for, but medieval gardens did play a subtle role in the social life of the time. Royalty and noblemen didn't marry for love; marriage was a contract designed to bring wealth, property, power and position to the family. Consequently, innocent flirtations played a big part in court life but, as you couldn't risk putting a foot wrong, knights followed the rules of courtly behaviour (a sort of early etiquette). A sound knowledge of social graces such as dancing, singing, poetry and music was an essential part of the knight's armoury, and much use of it took place in the garden. To add to the atmosphere, troupes of strolling musicians and players – troubadours – travelled the country putting on live entertainment, with the emphasis on romantic themes, again in the garden. Paradise re-created? Well, call it paradise cleaned up.

EDWARD III AND WINDSOR

From its earth and timber beginnings under William the Conqueror, Windsor Castle was steadily extended and improved by a string of monarchs. It was Henry I who really started the ball rolling by adding decent domestic quarters and buying the land outside the castle, which became the King's gardens in 1110. Henry II converted Windsor into a palace, upgraded the accommodation and added a Great Hall for regal-style entertaining. Richard the Lionheart spent £30 creating the King's herber inside the castle walls near the end of his reign, but

ABOVE: *Edward III made the castle and gardens at Windsor his great project.*

as he wasn't at home much, it's probably about all you could expect of him.

Henry III was another great builder, who built Westminster Abbey and also made further additions to Windsor. Edward II put new turf benches around the grounds, for which thousands of turves were cut specially. But it was Edward III who made Windsor his major project. He extended it enormously to turn it into his seat of government, spending £50,000 on improvements – an absolute fortune.

Prior to Edward's wedding in 1338 to Philippa of Hainault – a keen gardener – a great deal of work was done in the gardens at Windsor, and at the manor of Shene in Surrey. (This had originally been bought by Edward I, and passed down through the generations along with the rest of the steadily mounting collection of royal properties.) Edward converted the manor house into a royal palace, complete with a moat and an enormous deer park stretching as far as the river at Kew. A pavilion was built on a nearby island in the river Thames as a special hideaway for the happy couple. The manor of Shene would eventually become Richmond Palace, and part of the land would end up as Kew Gardens.

It was during Edward III's reign that rosemary first arrived in England. As a wedding gift his wife received a parcel of rosemary cuttings from her mother, along with the medieval equivalent of an instruction leaflet. As a result, rosemary became very popular for a wide variety of medicinal, cosmetic and decorative purposes.

One of the best descriptions of the gardens at Windsor Castle in the early fifteenth century comes from James I of Scotland, who was imprisoned there from 1413 to 1424. He'd been captured from a stranded ship at the age of 12, and seems to have spent much of his time writing poetry. From this we know that his cell overlooked an enclosure with hawthorn hedges, alleys, lots of flowers and dense greenery, including 'sweet juniper', with a bower and nightingales singing. He was clearly let out occasionally, as it was while walking beneath the tower at Windsor that he met his future wife, Jane Beaufort, the daughter of John of Gaunt.

PLANTS IN SICKNESS AND IN HEALTH

Long before they were valued for their decorative properties, plants were a vital part of the family medicine chest; being used to promote general wellbeing and as specific cures for all manner of aches, pains and complaints.

Plants and Medicine

Medieval medical problems were many and varied. There was 'falling sickness' (epilepsy), ague (fever) and malaria (which was sometimes contracted by Crusaders, but was in any case endemic in parts of England, especially the damp Kentish marshes). St Anthony's fire was ergotism, caused by eating grain infected with a fungus that looked like mouse droppings among the ears of corn. People also suffered from the bites of mad dogs and venomous serpents, and evil spells – these being superstitious times when anything that wasn't understood was usually explained away as witchcraft.

The best medicine at the time was that dispensed by monks who had trained in herbal medicine.

The doctrine of signatures

Many early herbal remedies were discovered by trial and error, but in medieval times God was believed to give us a clue by marking some plants to advertise their curative powers. Self-heal has a sickle-shaped mark, showing that it could be used to cure cuts; the flowers of skullcap were the same shape as the human skull to suggest that it was good for afflictions of the head, such as insomnia. Best known of all is pulmonaria, or lungwort, whose spotty leaves indicate it could treat lung diseases, such as tuberculosis. The results were no doubt mixed.

HERALDIC EMBLEMS

A handful of favourite flowers really made it big as
heraldic emblems.

Broom

According to legend, Geoffrey of Anjou camped on a
heath on his way to a battle and stuck a sprig of yellow
broom flowers into his helmet. He was easily
recognized by the '*Planta genista*' flower he wore, which
became the 'badge' of his descendants. Geoffrey
married the only daughter of Henry I of England, and
their son became the next king, Henry II. Henry and his
descendants kept Geoffrey's nickname of Plantagenet
as their surname until the line ended with Richard III.

Thistle

The thistle is said to have become the Scottish insignia
after a Danish soldier, in a party of invaders who
attacked under cover of darkness, trod on a thistle. His
ensuing howl of pain gave the game away, allowing the
Scots to slaughter the Danes.

Iris

Fleur-de-lys is a corruption of *fleur de luce* or *fleur de
Louis*, and is a stylized form of the common wild iris
that grows in swampy ground. In fifth-century France,
so the story goes, King Clovis was retreating from a
battle when he was cut off by a river. He was able to
lead the remains of his army to safety by following the
irises, which showed where the water was shallow. In
gratitude, he adopted the flower as his emblem, and in
the twelfth century it was taken up by Louis VII.

LEFT: *The fleur-de-lys design originates from
the common wild iris.*

Roses

At the time of Henry VII's marriage to Elizabeth, a rose
bush growing in a Wiltshire monastery garden suddenly
started producing red-and-white-striped blooms, when
previously they'd always been just one colour. It was
consequently called 'York and Lancaster', in honour of
the two families. The Tudors later adopted a rose as the
emblem of England. Their stylized heraldic rose was
diplomatically made up from the outer petals of the
Red Rose of Lancaster (*Rosa gallica* var. *officinalis*)
wrapped round the centre of the White Rose of York
(*Rosa* x *alba*). It became a familiar feature in
architecture as well as heraldry. Technically it's
Rosa x *damascena* var. *versicolor* and it is still available
from specialist rose growers. It grows roughly 5ft x 5ft
with flowers that are striped and mottled in several
shades of pink. The catalogue of a famous rose grower
describes it as more of a collector's piece than a plant
with real garden merit.

Their 'customers' would have been noble families who could afford their fees – everyone else paid a visit to the local 'wise woman', who knew about herbs, or relied on home-grown cures for day-to-day problems. Pellitory root (*Anacyclus pyrethrum*) was chewed for toothache, and self-heal or carpenter's herb (*Prunella vulgaris*) was grown to treat bruises and wounds.

But the big scourge of the time was the Black Death or bubonic plague. It arrived on fleas carried by black rats that escaped from a ship which arrived from the Continent and docked at Weymouth in 1348. The plague swept through England in several waves over 300 years, reducing the population to under 3 million (it's nearly 60 million today) and resulting in 1,000 villages being abandoned. 'Lost villages' can still be spotted from the air in dry summers: all that remains are long-buried foundations under fields.

The net result of the Black Death was such a severe shortage of agricultural labourers that much land fell out of cultivation, orchards and vineyards were neglected, and wages for labourers rose. By then, being a gardener at a noble house or royal palace would have been a very good job.

Plants and the Roots of Heraldry

Picture the scene. It's the Middle Ages, and there you are on a battlefield. Everyone is got up in helmets and chain mail, and they all look exactly the same… so in the heat of battle, how do you know whose head to chop off?

The Welsh found themselves in just that situation in the fifth century while having a spat with the Saxons, so to solve the problem they pulled leeks from nearby cottage gardens and stuck them in their helmets. The Saxons, not being in on the game, mistakenly slaughtered large numbers of their own men. Well, that's the story anyway.

History is full of myths about plants saving the day and ending up as 'mascots'. Eventually, more macho heraldic emblems, such as lions, appeared as coats of arms painted on shields – easier than picking flowers, particularly out of season. What's more, you could then use them decoratively as architectural features all around the house, and since you were now firmly in the realms of fantasy, there was nothing to stop you from incorporating all sorts of mythical beasts, such as unicorns and griffins.

As various families intermarried, split up or changed sides, they might divide their escutcheon (heraldic shield) into quarters and have a different emblem in each. After a few generations, things could become quite complicated.

The Wars of the Roses were fought from 1455 to 1485 between the rival houses of York (whose emblem was a white rose) and Lancaster (represented by a red rose). Both believed they had a legitimate claim to the throne. The wars claimed the lives of 80 noblemen and 100,000 'common soldiers', who all wore the appropriate flower on their helmets. The conflict ended with the death of the last of the Plantagenets – Richard III – on Bosworth Field, and the warring factions were eventually united by the marriage of Henry Tudor (of Lancaster) to Elizabeth, the eldest daughter of Edward IV (of York), who together founded the great Tudor dynasty.

High points in horticulture

Caxton invented his printing process and produced the first printed book in 1477, so for the first time books could be mass-produced at a price that allowed information to be more widely distributed among the educated nobility. Previously manuscripts had been laboriously copied by hand, which restricted their circulation mainly to scholars studying in monastic libraries.

POWER GARDENING UNDER THE TUDORS

HOUSE OF TUDOR

Henry VII 1485–1509

Henry VIII 1509–47

Edward VI 1547–53

Jane 10–19 July 1553

Mary I 1553–58

Elizabeth I 1558–1603

OPPOSITE ABOVE: Tudor garden design was strongly influenced by sport, plants and elegant hedging.

OPPOSITE BELOW: Montacute House in Somerset is a beautiful example of an Elizabethan garden and shows how royal taste influenced design.

After his victory at the battle of Bosworth in 1485, which ended the Wars of the Roses, Henry Tudor was crowned as Henry VII. The following year he diplomatically married Elizabeth of York, which united the two rival families and brought peace to the country at last.

The first outcome of peaceful times was that gardens no longer needed to be fortified. Henry's big unsung contribution to gardening was to order the defensive outer walls that enclosed the 'pleasaunces' round castles to be demolished, which meant that gardens could easily be enlarged. With no wars to take up their time and money, powerful landowners no longer needed to produce enough fruit and vegetables to feed their households, and for the first time in history they could afford the luxury of decorative surroundings. It was all systems go for gardening.

HENRY VII AND THE NEW BIG THING

Henry took his job seriously. Using the medieval Palace of Westminster as his London base, he not only kept a lid on fractious nobles, but also worked hard and was careful with money. When you consider that he'd started with a country that was practically bankrupt after being at war for 30 years, he did well to fill the coffers and have enough over to invest in the royal gardens.

A bad fire had almost completely destroyed the royal manor house at Shene on the river Thames in 1497, so Henry had it rebuilt and luxuriously furnished, creating a new royal residence – Richmond Palace – based on the style of a smart French chateau. It became his favourite home.

The garden, naturally, came in for a major makeover too. As well as putting in enclosed herbers, a privy garden and covered walkways, something completely different was tried out underneath the King's bedroom windows – knot gardens, made of dwarf evergreens outlined in sand and decorated with 3-D heraldic beasts. Henry didn't know it at the time, but his descendants would pick up his novel gardening themes and make much more of them. Knot gardens were to become the Big New Thing of the Tudor era, starting a style that would last for centuries, and heraldic beasts would become the Tudor equivalent of bedding plants, which wouldn't arrive till Victorian times.

Henry also developed the concept of garden leisure, creating from the old medieval 'pleasaunce' what you'd think of today as almost an 'amusement park' at the bottom of the garden. Far away from the house, he put up purpose-made outbuildings in which his family, household and guests could play chess, cards and dice. He also constructed bowling alleys, tennis courts and butts for archery, all surrounded by raised galleries from which onlookers could watch the fun and games.

Henry no doubt enjoyed the improved accommodation as much as anyone – there's no point in being king if you can't push the boat out a bit occasionally. But the big reason for giving Richmond Palace a makeover was to have it ready for the arrival of Catherine of Aragon, who was coming to England from Spain in 1501 to marry Henry VII's eldest son and heir to the throne – Prince Arthur. The youngsters had been betrothed since the prince was two, but fate took a hand and Arthur died. Not to be thwarted, Catherine set to and

The privy garden at
Richmond Palace (below)
was laid out by Henry Tudor
as part of a bigger design
which influenced Henry
VIII's showpiece garden at
Hampton Court (opposite).

Privy gardens

*A privy garden had
nothing to do with an
outside loo: it was a
garden for the royal
family to have some
privacy. The word 'privy'
is archaic, but survives
in institutions such as
the Privy Council and
the Privy Purse – the
monarch's advisers and
his State-provided
spending money.*

married the next in line to the throne, Henry, who
became Henry VIII. As it turned out, he was quite a
gardener, too.

MAGNIFICENCE AND EXTRAVAGANCE UNDER HENRY VIII

Henry VIII inherited a kingdom that, thanks to his
father, was flourishing. Now that noble families were
no longer at each other's throats all the time they
could amuse themselves by building magnificent
country houses, decorating them extravagantly and
making superb gardens with state-of-the-art sports
facilities – which they threw themselves into with
great gusto. Henry was a very good sportsman, keen

on hunting, jousting and tennis (the 'real' sort,
where the ball runs along roof beams), and it's
claimed that he was one of the best archers in the
land – though not quite so keen on work.

As Henry got older he acquired a playboy lifestyle,
overeating took its toll and his womanizing got out
of hand. His competitive personality made him
increasingly power-crazed, until he simply had to
come top at everything – gardening included – at
any cost. He felt compelled to outdo all his high-
ranking nobles to stop them getting ideas above
their station. But what really concerned him was
finding ways to outshine the French king, Francis I,
who was already well known for his extravagant
lifestyle, his elegant court and his stunning gardens
at Fontainebleau. One thing Henry desperately
wanted was a garden that would leave Francis's in
the shade.

On the surface England looked peaceful and
prosperous, but behind the scenes ruthless back-
stabbing was rife, as nobles jousted for position.
Careers rose and fell, and heads rolled. Under
Henry VIII, gardening became a blood sport.

The business with Hampton Court was
particularly sordid. Henry's penchant for having fun
when he should be working meant that he turned
most of his affairs of state over to his chum and
reliable right-hand man, Cardinal Wolsey.

Wolsey was an ambitious cleric, who thought that
owning a stately country pile would be a great career
boost as he'd be able to entertain the King and all
the official hangers-on in style, so in 1514 he took on
Hampton Court. But first the place needed a bit of
work. Keen on creating a classic look, he brought in
2,500 Italian workmen to enlarge the house. But as

is the way with building projects, the job 'grew' and Wolsey ended up with a 1,000-room mansion with purpose-built royal apartments, all decorated in lavish style. By 1520, the new improved Hampton Court was ready for guests and, according to plan, the King was a frequent visitor.

The trouble was, the more Henry saw of Hampton Court, the less he liked his own houses. Wolsey had definitely over-egged it.

Henry and Wolsey started falling out over trivial things, but the sparks finally flew when Henry wanted a divorce from wife number one (Catherine of Aragon) in order to marry Anne Boleyn. When Wolsey couldn't square it with the Pope, he felt obliged to make Henry a gift of Hampton Court to save face. But it was too late, and Wolsey was arrested for treason. Luckily for him, he died of natural causes before he could lose his head.

This left Henry, in 1525, the owner of Hampton Court. Although the place was already palatial, he spent a fortune on further improvements, paying particular attention to the garden. Without dramatically altering the original medieval layout, he 'borrowed' the gimmicks his father had tried on a small scale at Richmond, and which the new French king (Louis XII) had at Fontainebleau... but on a much bigger and more magnificent scale than anyone had ever seen before. Hampton Court was to be his big showpiece garden, and the envy of Europe.

Henry's Hampton Court Gardens

In 1533 Henry VIII started work on his three big projects at Hampton Court: the privy garden, the mount garden and the pond garden.

What's there today?

Nothing of Henry's Hampton Court garden remains today, as it was all swept away when William and Mary brought in Sir Christopher Wren to give the place a massive makeover in 1689. The privy garden on view now is the William and Mary version, which was recently restored.

BELOW AND OPPOSITE: *Henry VIII was a great all-round sportsman and hunting was one of his favourite pastimes – so, naturally, deer parks were incorporated into his palaces, including Hampton Court.*

St James's Park

In 1531 Henry VIII bought 185 acres of land close to Whitehall Palace to use as a deer park. It was named St James's Park after a hospice dedicated to St James, which had previously stood on the site. Henry built a hunting lodge that was later extended to become St James's Palace, and the deer park would be redeveloped as gardens by later monarchs (see pages 75 and 93).

The privy garden was usually close to the royal family's private apartments, quite separate from the posh state gardens which were used to entertain and impress visiting dignitaries. Henry's privy garden was laid out under the windows of his private apartments so that he could look down on it from above, and was planted in the very latest fashion – as a knot garden. The winding patterns of clipped dwarf evergreens were brightened up with a menagerie of wooden heraldic beasts, colourfully painted and with gold highlights. They were the king's beasts, which included dragons, greyhounds, griffins and tigers, each clutching a shield bearing coats of arms, and sitting on top of short poles pushed into the ground. To keep the beasts safely caged, the beds were edged with low green-and-white-painted wooden rails, which eventually became a hallmark of fashionable Tudor gardens. The same colours and heraldic symbols were used on flags and in architecture, this being a time of great pageantry.

The mount was vertical gardening, Tudor style. An artificial hill was made for Henry, using a quarter of a million bricks for the foundations, with earth piled up on top to make a cone-shaped 'garden' planted with roses and evergreens, through which a path spiralled its way up to the top. Along the path were more heraldic beasts and green-and-white rails, and at the very top sat a three-storey banqueting hall, with a decorative lead roof and so many large glass windows that Henry referred to it as a 'lantern arbour', in which to sit and enjoy the views.

The pond yard was Henry's water feature, all formal, rectangular fish ponds. With no running water on tap, he hired labourers to fill the pond with water baled out of the river at dead of night, using – so it's rumoured – just kitchen pots and pans.

Henry naturally added sports facilities to the grounds at Hampton Court. He put in tennis courts, bowling alleys, a tiltyard for jousting and a 2,000-acre deer park for hunting. Having taken a shine to

Wife trouble

When Henry took over Hampton Court Wolsey's coat of arms featured everywhere. It was soon replaced with Henry's, which had to be constantly retouched as he changed wives.

Wife number three, Jane Seymour, bore his only son, Edward (later Edward VI), at Hampton Court but died shortly afterwards.

Wife number five, Catherine Howard, was held there awaiting her trial on trumped-up adultery charges. When she tried to see Henry, guards dragged her away. Her ghost is said to haunt the passageways – screams and sudden temperature drops were reported. Ghost-hunters have been in with thermal imaging equipment, but believe that Catherine is merely a draught.

Wolsey's Italian-style decoration indoors, Henry went in for classical stonework in the gardens. He ordered marble columns, statues and a joke fountain designed to drench passers-by, based on an original idea much loved by the ancient Romans. Sundials were just coming in, so Henry sent for 20 to be dotted around the gardens.

Henry's Lost Gardens

England had been a Catholic country until 1535, but after his divorce from Catherine of Aragon created a rift with the Pope, Henry VIII established the Church of England with himself as its head, and set about seizing the monasteries. In this way he was able to kill two birds with one stone. Selling off monastery buildings and lands raised cash for the Crown – it was running short because of his heavy spending habits – and also made him popular by enabling a lot of nouveau-riche social climbers to elevate themselves to the ranks of the landed gentry.

The spin-off was a big boom in country house and garden building. Many monasteries were left intact and refurbished as grand new homes, and their agricultural buildings were converted into smart manor houses with grounds. Some monastic buildings were just left to fall down, and were then pulled to pieces so that the stone could be recycled as building material. Plants from the old monastery gardens were also pilfered, so for the first time medicinal plants started appearing in decorative gardens. Henry also helped himself to these. He sent some gardeners to a Carthusian monastery he'd just axed to swipe some trees for re-homing at Hampton Court.

He used what history books now call the dissolution of the monasteries as a good excuse to 'acquire' Syon House, a convent just outside London that he'd taken a shine to, and in 1539 he threw out the resident nuns. The house stayed in royal hands for only a few years; after Henry's death in 1547 his son (Edward VI) gave it to his uncle, Edward Seymour, who reappears later in the story.

'Acquiring' other people's properties became something of a habit with Henry, especially if he felt a twinge of rivalry. His *modus operandi* was a simple one: to find fault with the owner – treason was always a safe bet – seize his estates for the Crown and behead the miscreant. In this way Henry gained quite a goodly number of country homes, castles and gardens. Some, like Syon House, didn't remain in royal ownership for long because grand houses and gardens were good currency for trading favours, and others have since vanished completely.

The magnificence of the lost gardens can be learnt of only from contemporary reports:

Thornbury Castle was a huge, fortified country house in Gloucester built by Thomas Stafford, a nobleman who was a favourite courtier of Henry's in 1511 at the start of his reign. Stafford was an ambitious man who entertained on a staggering scale. Unfortunately, he overdid it a bit and, since he had royal blood in his veins, Henry scented a potential rival. Stafford was found guilty of treason and executed, and Henry took over the house.

Whitehall Palace was originally a Thames-side home in central London called York Place, and was owned by Cardinal Wolsey before it fell into Henry's hands

LEFT: Nonsuch Palace was Henry's challenge to the splendour of Fontainebleau, but, unfortunately, he never had the chance to enjoy it in its finished state.

at the same time as he 'acquired' Hampton Court. Since most of the Palace of Westminster had burnt down in 1512 (medieval buildings were as flammable as tinderboxes), Henry improved York Place and turned it into the Palace of Whitehall, which became his new government headquarters. There Henry created a typical new-Tudor garden, very much in the style of the privy garden at Hampton Court. Being right in the heart of London, Whitehall was to prove a useful royal residence for many monarchs until it burnt down in 1698.

Chelsea was the home of the saintly Sir Thomas More, author of *Utopia*, a work that describes how to run the perfect state – nothing like Henry's. Appointed to succeed Cardinal Wolsey, he didn't stay long in the job as he wanted to spend more time with his family. Meanwhile he'd built himself a superb house with a garden and a small farm in a little village called Chelsea. Being handily located for the city, Sir Thomas could step straight from his garden into a boat and cruise into work at Whitehall. Henry

was a regular visitor, and greatly admired More's splendid gardens. Then the inevitable happened – yes, you've guessed....

Nonsuch was Henry VIII's biggest and most ambitious project by far – a palace and garden that he intended to start from scratch to outshine the French king's sensational spreads at Fontainebleau and Chambord. The name was chosen quite deliberately: there was to be nonsuch like it anywhere, and Henry wanted the world to know it.

Work began in 1538 on a piece of ground in Surrey, between Cheam and Ewell. Henry's dream house was to be a wedding cake-type confection with all the trimmings. The garden was loosely inspired by the Italian Renaissance style that Henry had taken a fancy to, thanks to Cardinal Wolsey's ideas at Hampton Court, complete with kitchen garden and deer park. Although a good start was made on the garden Nonsuch was only half-finished by the time Henry died. His eventual successor, Elizabeth I, would, however, enjoy it.

Tudor Plants

ABOVE: *Jasminum officinale was a popular choice of plant in Tudor times; strategically positioned, it added scent to gardens and interiors.*

Gardeners during Henry VIII's reign had much the same range of plants as their ancestors, though they used them in different ways to make fashionable features, such as knot gardens. But now a few foreign plants were starting to come into the country.

Flowers

Highly scented flowers, such as lilies, jasmine, carnations and pinks, remained popular throughout Tudor times. Carnations and pinks were sometimes grown in pots and stood in troughs outside windows. Aromatic evergreen herbs were the favourite plants for making knot gardens; the air-freshening effect in the bedchambers that overlooked them was welcome as plumbing was still medieval.

New arrivals included antirrhinum (known as 'broad calf's snout'), winter cherry, which came over from Turkey, and French marigold *Tagetes patula* (known as 'velvet flower') which arrived from Mexico.

A big influx of Huguenots arrived from the Low Countries from 1540 onwards, fleeing religious persecution. They settled mainly in East Anglia, and among them were talented gardeners who brought with them new skills and new plants. They were responsible for the arrival of cultivated hybrids of narcissi, hyacinths, roses and pinks, when previously all we'd had were wild species. These new arrivals and their plants were the origins of 'florists', who rose to fame in the seventeenth century as breeders and exhibitors of collector's flowers.

Fruit and vegetables

Always well known for his healthy appetite, Henry VIII was very keen on fruit, which was cooked in a variety of ways but rarely eaten raw in Tudor times for fear of dysentery. Since the choice available in England at the time was fairly poor, the King sent his head fruiterer, Richard Harris, over to France to bring back some new varieties. In 1533 he established a 100-acre fruit garden at Teynham, near what is now Sittingbourne in Kent. It was described as 'the cherry garden and the apple orchard of Kent', from which Kent took its name as the 'Garden of England'. Grafting made it possible to propagate the new varieties reasonably rapidly, and soon more orchards were being planted throughout the northern half of the county.

Trained fruit trees also became popular for growing on walls and over bowers in gardens. Henry had strawberries grown for the table at Hampton Court, and apricot trees were brought back from mainland Europe especially for his new garden at Nonsuch. At first they were known as 'hasty peaches' because they ripened earlier than the real thing.

Vegetables began to come back into fashion during Henry's reign. Although we tend to think of him as a roast-meat man, wading into swan drumsticks at banquets, it was he who first introduced the idea of eating vegetables with meat instead of as a separate course.

Broad beans had by now been introduced, and cucumbers had been reintroduced – they'd originally come to Britain with the Romans but, being frost-tender, had soon died out again. Henry was keen on cucumbers (which may have been something to do with rarity value) and plants were grown specially for him all year round in greenhouses heated by hotbeds of fermenting manure. Since glass couldn't be made in greenhouse-sized sheets at the time, Henry's 'glasshouses' were most likely glazed with mica – a technique thought up by the Romans – but, even so, this was very much a rich man's hobby. Vegetable-growers among the newly arrived Huguenot refugees settled around London and set up thriving market gardens supplying the now-expanding city.

RIGHT: *Tudor gardens marked the emergence of the knot garden – elegant and intricate flowerbeds that added year-round interest. The style is still used today, as at this garden at Barnsley House, Gloucestershire.*

FEATURES OF TUDOR GARDENS

Tudor gardens were a much more glamorous version of the underlying medieval design. The big innovation was the knot garden, which remained popular for two centuries, but other features surfaced too.

Knot Gardens

Knot gardens were the latest fashion in flowerbeds during Tudor times. They were the logical 'next step' from the raised beds of medieval castle gardens, and, like them, were designed to be placed under the bedchambers of the house where the occupants could look down on them from above.

Whereas medieval flowerbeds had been simple shapes – squares or rectangles edged with low woven willow 'fences' – Tudor knot gardens were complicated and intricate patterns edged with clipped miniature 'hedges'. Being made from dwarf evergreens, knots were the first real attempt at giving a garden all-year-round interest.

The earliest knots were outlined with thrift (*Armeria maritima*), which grew wild around parts of the British coastline, though later a wide range of scented evergreen herbs, such as hyssop, lavender, rosemary and thyme, were used. (Today's first choice for edging paths or beds – dwarf box – wasn't introduced until 1595.)

Plants for knot gardens had to stand up to close clipping, which was done every month to keep the intricate outlines in shape, but were also chosen for their scent, which partly compensated for the lack of colour. The clippings from newly-trimmed knot

ABOVE: *The medieval mount*
also received the Tudor
treatment and, in these new
times of peace, found an
ornamental place in gardens.

gardens were often strewn on the floor inside the house as natural air-fresheners.

An open knot was a simple geometrical pattern of evergreens only, in which all paths led to the centre, with the spaces in-between the plants filled with brick dust, sand, gravel, coal dust or crushed minerals to provide year-round colour in the absence of bedding plants. This type of knot garden often had painted rails around it for colour, or was sometimes edged with strips of lead, roof tiles, wooden boards or even rows of old meat knuckle-bones stood on end.

A closed knot was a much fancier design, often outlining the shape of heraldic beasts or a family crest, the spaces filled with a tightly packed mixture of flowers. Virtually the only available flowers that could be used this way were spring bulbs – daffodils and hyacinths – and spring wild flowers, such as cowslips and primroses, so such colour as there was

would be pretty short-lived and seasonal. The evergreen outline still created the main interest.

Mazes in Tudor times were not the tall hedge type – a seventeenth-century ideal – but a low maze pattern, outlined in short, compact plants, growing in a rectangular bed that you could walk around without the bother of having to find your way out – something like pedestrian hopscotch.

Galleries

A variation on medieval cloisters, galleries were walks, enclosed by trelliswork walls, that connected various parts of the garden – something like a pergola but more closed in. The galleries in Henry VIII's gardens were used as 'privy ways' that allowed the royal family to reach the chapel or other favourite places without having to hobnob with 'outsiders'.

Mounts

Like knot gardens, mounts were direct descendants of features in medieval castle gardens, where watch-towers started life as mounds of soil piled up against the castle walls, from which guards used to spot invaders and shoot them.

In their new ornamental form, mounts could be placed in the centre of the garden, where they commanded a good view over features such as knot gardens and ponds, or close to the edge of the garden, where you could look into the surrounding deer park and watch the hunt.

The popular height for a Tudor mount was roughly 30 feet; it had a spiral path leading up to a flat top, where there might be an open-air arbour with a turf seat. But all the best mounts, like Henry VIII's at Hampton Court, had a more sophisticated

building on top: a banqueting house – not to be confused with a banqueting hall as the garden version wasn't used for feasts, but was more like a summer-house.

Making a mount was a great way to get rid of garden rubbish, as one John Worlidge sagely observed in 1700.

GARDENING IN THE GOLDEN AGE

Elizabeth I was a phenomenally powerful queen who steered England through one of the most exciting times in its history. Wealth was escalating, country-house-building and garden-making reached an all-time peak, merchant seafarers were trading with the world and bringing back valuable treasures, and the trickle of new plants coming into the country increased to a steady flow. Fans of art and literature were spoilt for choice, scientific knowledge was advancing and gardening books were on the increase. Gardeners had never had it so good.

Under the circumstances almost any monarch would have been popular, but Elizabeth was a superstar to her subjects. Being single, she used feminine wiles to get her own way. Her admirers couldn't do enough to impress her while she kept them dangling, but she never married. It was all a big power game, and she ruthlessly exploited the advantages of remaining the Virgin Queen.

Knowing Elizabeth's fondness for gardens, the best way ahead for ambitious courtiers was to create a truly magnificent country estate with extravagant gardens and all the trimmings, then invite the

Where to see a Tudor garden

Genuine Tudor gardens, kept exactly as they were without alteration, haven't lasted the course, but at Southampton a good reproduction has been made just behind the Tudor House Museum (see page 54). The house was once the home of Henry VIII's Lord Chief Justice, and the garden – though only small – is quite authentic.

William Turner

ABOVE: Borage (Borago officinalis) is just one of the many herbs mentioned in Turner's New Herball.

Science was moving at a faster pace by now, and towards the end of Henry VIII's reign, botany branched off from the natural sciences, led by the 'father of English botany', William Turner.

Turner had originally trained as a medical doctor, and then became personal physician to Edward Seymour, the Lord Protector (the chap who was given Syon House by Edward VI after Henry VIII's death). Both men were keen on plants and Turner travelled widely around Europe with his boss. As a result, he started the first-ever herbarium – a collection of dried botanical specimens – and produced a book of Continental plant names and their English equivalents.

Turner kept up to date with all the latest developments in botany, and took every opportunity to study plants – he was in regular contact with the world's first botanical garden, at Padua, just outside Venice, in Italy. He compiled his *New Herball*, detailing the medicinal uses of plants, and dedicated it to Queen Elizabeth I, who had by then taken the throne.

Queen and her circle of courtiers to stay and really pile on the flattery. The way Elizabeth saw it, the more effort and expense generous hosts spent on her hospitality, the more loyalty they were showing towards her and, being practical about it, the less she had to fork out for herself.

As a result, there was a great flurry of rebuilding. Old houses were expensively done up. New country houses were sycophantically built in the shape of the letter 'E' for Elizabeth. Gardens became ever more complicated. Knot gardens were still the main feature, but now upwardly mobile Elizabethans also needed to add new features, such as terraces, alleys of pleached trees, topiary, 'forthrights' (see page 53) and the latest Italian-style stoneware to keep one jump ahead of the competition. As for plants, anything new – naturally – was 'in'.

Gardens for Gloriana

No opportunity was spared to attract a royal visit and thereby gain the power and influence that came with royal approval. A great garden was the fast track to success... but things didn't always work out quite as intended.

Robert Dudley, Earl of Leicester, pulled out the stops to impress Elizabeth with the fashionable garden he made at Kenilworth Castle. It was only an acre, but crammed with all the latest must-have Elizabethan garden features – a terrace, knot gardens, virginal white heraldic beasts perched on posts, Italianate obelisks and a romantic bower. When the Queen came to stay she complained that she couldn't see the formal gardens from her bedchamber, so Dudley promptly hired a gang of gardeners to make one especially for her, right under her window. Elizabeth and Dudley became very close, and the court was rife with gossip about their liaison. Some worried that she might finally take the plunge and marry him, thus losing much of her mystique and with it her power. But the moment passed.

Elizabeth's Lord Chancellor, Sir Christopher Hatton, was not so lucky. He practically bankrupted himself building a superb house, Holdenby House in Northamptonshire, with one aim in mind – to impress and entertain the Queen. The gardens were outstanding, with not one but two mounts, a three-storey banqueting house and a rosery (Elizabethan for rose garden). When he died, almost ten years after it was finished, the Queen had still not been anywhere near it; it had all been a complete waste of time.

ABOVE: Kenilworth Castle in Warwickshire was the home of Elizabeth I's favourite courtier, Robert Dudley, Earl of Leicester, and was lavishly laid out to impress the Queen. Although the castle is now in ruins, the Tudor garden has been reconstructed in front of the original Norman keep.

Virgin's bowers

The Elizabethan diarist John Evelyn was thought to have coined the name 'Virgin's bower' for the clematis as a bit of royal flattery. Clematis were popular for bowers at the time, and although only a few species were grown, history records three varieties: Clematis alpina, *the fragrant* Clematis flammula *and the nodding* Clematis rehderiana.

OPPOSITE: The gardens at Montacute House included a terrace – a new idea for Elizabethans that reflected their love of Italianate features.

Lord Burleigh (William Cecil), Elizabeth's secretary of state, was a keen gardener who spent a fortune creating a stunning garden at his modest country house, Theobalds (pronounced 'Tib-balds') in Hertfordshire. Elizabeth often visited, complete with her large circle of attendants and hangers-on. On one occasion she complained that her bedchamber was too small, so Lord Burleigh had it enlarged for her, and from then on the dutiful courtier was constantly pestered to keep extending and upgrading the house until it ended up as a massive country mansion. It was fortunate for Lord Burleigh that Elizabeth's envy did not approach that of her father, or Burleigh might have been in serious trouble.

The garden at Theobalds was said to have been the inspiration behind Francis Bacon's essay 'Of Gardens', the gist of which is that gardens should be art forms, with no expense spared. That description certainly fitted Theobalds. The garden contained all the most fashionable Tudor features, some of which could be toured by boat via the extensive water gardens, plus a summer-house with 12 marble Roman emperors sitting round a stone table – which must have made the seating plan a bit of a challenge. Lead cisterns reputedly housing shoals of fish were used for watering, and the whole garden was supervised by John Gerard, author of the famous *Herball* or *General Historie of Plants*, of whom more later (see page 52).

Elizabeth much preferred travelling and being entertained to staying at home and doing up her own gardens. But she did dabble a bit.

At Whitehall Palace she ordered a flock of painted and gilded heraldic beasts carrying her own coat of arms for the privy garden, plus some sundials which were very fashionable. She also put in a bowling green – the up-and-coming garden sport.

Nonsuch was her favourite garden, but after Henry VIII's death and the subsequent squabbling over the succession that occupied the years before Elizabeth took the helm, the property had been bought by Henry FitzAlan, Earl of Arundel. He spent a fortune finishing off Henry's dream garden, sticking quite closely to the original plans. According to contemporary descriptions, there was a pleasure garden containing life-like artificial animals (so much less trouble than a real menagerie) as well as all the latest sports facilities, including the now almost compulsory bowling green and a hedge maze.

Elizabeth visited Nonsuch often, lapping up FitzAlan's hospitality. After he died she bought it back, and it remained in royal hands until Charles II's time.

FEATURES OF ELIZABETHAN GARDENS

The Italian touches that Cardinal Wolsey first introduced at Hampton Court began to bear fruit, and Italy started to be looked on as something of a style-setter. Elizabeth spoke Italian fluently, and noblemen commonly packed their sons off on a visit to Italy to complete their education. There they would have seen villas whose grounds were packed with classical-style fountains, statues and urns that re-created the heyday of ancient Greece and Rome, and featured very different planting schemes from those at home.

OPPOSITE: *Mazes were a popular Elizabethan feature and were used as an amusement for visitors. This maze at Hatfield House has been restored to its original design and is open to the public.*

LITERARY WHO'S WHO

The Elizabethans were great writers, artists, scientists and thinkers, often all at once, and many of the big names of the day knew each other, with inevitable cross-pollination. Being so very fashionable, plants, gardens and gardening were popular themes in their work and discourse.

Francis Bacon

Although Francis Bacon started his career as a lawyer in 1576, as often happened at the time he branched out into other activities. He was also a scientist, philosopher and writer, best known for a volume of essays, published in 1597, that includes 'Of Gardens'. He eventually became Lord Chancellor to James I, who succeeded Elizabeth. Towards the end of his life he had a huge house and garden in London, but died of a chill after a failed attempt to invent frozen food by filling a chicken with ice.

John Gerard

Born in Cheshire in 1545, John Gerard trained as a barber-surgeon in London (barbers did a bit of surgery on the side in those days). He became interested in plants and was one of the first people in England to grow potatoes. His own garden at Gray's Inn Lane, in the then rural village of Holborn, was well stocked with plants we'd call weeds today – such as shepherds' purse – but at the time they had medicinal uses.

Gerard went to work for William Cecil (who later became Lord Burleigh) and managed the gardens at both Cecil's London home in the Strand and his country home, Theobalds, in Hertfordshire.

In 1599 he published his bestseller – *Herball* or *General Historie of Plants* (above right) – describing the medical and magical properties of plants. There wasn't much in it about gardening, and Mrs Gerard chipped in with a few contributions of her own for the benefit of lady readers. Gerard's *Herball* has remained a classic for centuries.

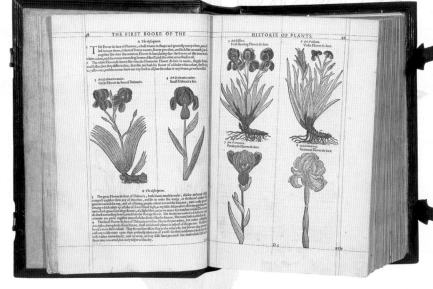

William Shakespeare

Born in Stratford in 1564, William Shakespeare received a grammar school education and seems to have been a bit of a handful. He married a woman eight years older than himself – Anne Hathaway – and left town suddenly after raiding the local deer park, to avoid unpleasant repercussions.

Moving to London, he joined a company of players and eventually became a partner in the Globe Theatre. He mingled with the literary world and had powerful friends at court, which must have been a help when he took up writing.

Shakespeare set several of his plays in gardens, and flowers and plant-lore figure in them frequently. John Gerard was a close neighbour of his, so it's quite likely that the two of them exchanged tips. On his retirement, Will moved back to Stratford and died of a chill after a drunken night out with some fellow creative talents.

The ideas they brought back began to alter the general layout of the garden. The basic Elizabethan garden was still based on the 'large square divided into four smaller ones' of medieval times, but now it was becoming very much more elaborate, with faint touches of classical Italian styling starting to creep in.

Along the back wall of the house would be a raised terrace, a platform from which to look out over the garden. From there, flights of steps took you down to ground level where long, straight walks – known as 'forthrights' – led forth into the garden at right angles from the terrace. These crossed with other paths running parallel to the terrace, so the garden looked like a giant chessboard, with each square containing a flowerbed, topiary, knot garden or some other popular Elizabethan feature. Further away from the house the ground became less formal, with orchards, fish ponds and all the usual sports facilities.

Walks were an important feature; they could be surfaced with turf, sand or low spreading herbs. Walks were often turned into shady alleys by planting trees alongside and training the branches out horizontally over a timber framework to make a leafy tunnel that met in the middle. This pleached alley or allée, as it was known, was more than just an idle gardening whim: pale skin was fashionable for well-bred ladies; only manual workers had a tan.

Arbours and banqueting halls gradually evolved into more sophisticated structures, such as gazebos (so called because you were supposed to place them where you could gaze out over a particularly good view). Arbours and gazebos often had plants growing

ABOVE: Topiary was an Italian fashion that was embraced with gusto by the Elizabethans, and books of engravings of inspirational designs were even published.

OPPOSITE: Hedging and topiary were popular features of Tudor gardens and added year-round structure and colour, as in this example at Tudor House, Southampton.

over them, and scarlet runners were used as ornamental climbers – we hadn't learnt to eat them yet. Tree arbours – which were fancy Elizabethan tree houses – were also made, and trees would be specially trained so that their branches grew to form natural rafters. One garden in Kent contained a lime tree with a tree house big enough to take 50 people.

Topiary and clipped hedges were popular. Topiary had been fashionable in grand Italian gardens since the fifteenth century, when the ancient Roman look came back into favour. It took time to reach England. Henry VIII had a fair amount of topiary at Hampton Court, but it wasn't made of the box or yew we'd use today. Rosemary was the popular topiary subject at the time; it was tied over a framework of willow twigs to form the outline of peacocks, or heraldic beasts such as greyhounds. Rosemary was also very popular for training as a wall shrub throughout Tudor times and, being slightly tender, was safer there and grew taller than out in the open. As in medieval times, serious hedging for surrounding gardens was generally made of hawthorn, blackthorn or the native small-leaved privet which were loosely referred to as 'quickset'.

Shakespeare's gardens

Shakespeare's birthplace in Stratford and Anne Hathaway's cottage are now essential stop-overs on the tourist trail. The birthplace has a collection of plants mentioned in Shakespeare's plays, and at his place of retirement – Nash House (right) – an Elizabethan-style garden has been re-created. The present garden at Anne Hathaway's cottage is, however, Victorian in style rather than Tudor.

Exploration and Gardening

Elizabethans were great adventurers, sailing the world in search of new trade routes to China and the Spice Islands, and the Queen was enthusiastic about the strange fruits, vegetables and exotic herbs that were being brought back.

Potatoes are popularly supposed to have been introduced from Virginia in America by Sir Walter Raleigh, but that idea has been discredited as the plant isn't thought to have been growing there at the time of his visit. Thanks to Christopher Columbus in 1492, the Spanish had colonized parts of South America, and their ships were always going to and from Europe. Potatoes were often taken on board as food on the return journeys, and were almost certainly growing in Spain before English explorers knew anything about them. From there they found their way to other parts of Europe. Some stories suggest potatoes arrived in England from coastal shipwrecks; others that they were already growing in Ireland. Walter Raleigh owned property in Ireland, so he may have brought some to England from there. It's also very likely that tubers trickled into the country from several sources at around the same time.

However their introduction happened, the first potatoes were a rarity tasted only by the very wealthiest members of society. The price was enormous, and, in common with a lot of expensive edible Elizabethan novelties, spuds were initially regarded as an aphrodisiac. It would be another 200 years before *Solanum tuberosum* was commonly grown by ordinary people.

ELIZABETHAN PLANTS

Long-distance exploration, increasing overseas trade and changing gardening tastes all helped to speed up the rate at which new plants arrived in Elizabethan gardens.

- New introductions included African marigold, martagon lilies, crown imperial fritillaries, and the hardy annuals love-in-a-mist (*Nigella*), larkspur and sunflowers.
- Descendants of the Huguenot refugees who'd arrived in Britain during Henry's reign were busy perfecting 'florist's flowers'. Their aim was to breed improved forms with double blooms, larger sizes, more perfect round shapes and regular markings.
- Vegetable-growing had an upturn under Henry VIII, and by Elizabethan times melons, pumpkins, gourds, marrows, cucumbers, parsnips and skirrets (a root veg we don't grow nowadays) were cultivated. Orange carrots had appeared instead of the medieval kinds, which were white. People also grew and used a huge range of salad herbs.
- Roses had increased enormously in popularity, and by 1560 up to 24 different species were available, including the smattering that had been around in medieval gardens.
- Elizabethan plants were given interesting common names, including: Flower armor – *Amaranthus* (love lies bleeding), Gillyflowers – carnations; Sops in wine – pinks; Dragons – tarragon; Poret – spring onions; Paggles – cowslips; Pompions – marrows; Eringo root – sea holly; Langdebiefe – borage; Indian cress – nasturtium; Coleworts – cabbages; Cowcumber – cucumber and Roser – rose (rosery – rose garden).

ABOVE: Lilium martagon – *a new introduction to gardens in Elizabethan England.*

ELIZABETHAN GARDENING ADVICE

Now that books were being more widely distributed, and written in English instead of Latin, all sorts of gardening advice was being put about – some good, some eccentric and some positively dubious. But at least it catered both for readers from the top drawer and those a little lower down in the pecking order. The following men were particularly influential in spreading advice to gardeners.

Thomas Hill

Born in 1529, Thomas Hill worked as a freelance writer covering all the popular topics of the day – astrology, cookery, psychology, medicine and gardening. He'd have been a gift to women's magazines if they'd had them then. In 1577 he produced his best-known work, *The Gardener's Labyrinth* (illustration above). This was a compilation of recycled gardening tips and hints from classical Roman authors, such as Varro, Columnella, Cato and Pliny the Elder, sprinkled with more current advice, including astrological gardening and medical notes.

Although there had been an earlier practical gardening book in English (brought out in late medieval times by the king's gardener), it is Hill's book that is always regarded as the first, and it was certainly the first to stand the test of time. Reprinted comparatively recently, it's a fascinating insight into early gardening techniques if you don't mind wrestling with the archaic English. But take some of the advice – such as blowing the left horn of an ox to dispel fog, or stuffing an owl heart into ants' nests to deter the pests – with a pinch of salt.

Thomas Tusser

Eton-educated Thomas Tusser (1515–80) was a schoolmaster, grazier and livestock trader from Essex, who loved music and poetry but was also a hands-on practical grower, or 'husbandman' as they were called. He was famous for his novel slant on gardening advice – he gave it in rhyme. His *500 Points of Good Husbandry*, published in 1580, was good practical advice aimed at the farm housewife who did all the day-to-day kitchen gardening. He covered all the usual jobs – sowing, planting and weeding, plus seasonal reminders – in easy-to-remember rhyming couplets that must have echoed round people's heads in the irritating way that advertising jingles do today. Take this advice for January: 'What greater crime, than loss of time?'

Tusser is full of good advice on which plants to use for different purposes; and it's fascinating to see how many decorative and culinary plants had crept into middle-class Elizabethan gardens, including:
- 25 essential herbs to grow in the garden for physic (meaning medicinal use).
- 17 herbs to still (i.e. distil) in summer.
- 21 strowing herbs, which were strewn on the floor of banqueting halls and bedchambers, and periodically swept up and replaced. This practice was common until well into the 16th century, and meadowsweet was a special favourite; don't forget, they didn't have carpets or vacuum cleaners, and their table manners were rudimentary.
- 20 herbs and sallet roots for sauce, 43 seeds and herbs for the kitchen and 9 herbs and roots to boil or to butter.
- 39 herbs, branches and flowers for windows and pots, including amaranthus (love lies bleeding), gillyflowers, sops in wine, campion, and also plants used for making tussie-mussies (nosegays), which were carried to take your mind off the pong as you walked in the streets.

Sir Hugh Platt

From a well-heeled Hertfordshire family, Sir Hugh Platt was an inventor and a keen gardener, who accumulated an immense knowledge of plants at his own three gardens, and through regular visits and correspondence with other gardeners.

He is the author of *Flora's Paradise*, but far more fun is his 1594 book *Delights for Ladies*, a collection of Elizabethan still-room secrets, which included 'recipts' (recipes) for using flowers, fruits and herbs for making your own elegant plant-potions. In it, readers learn how to make such delights as their own rose water, flower vinegars, pomanders, washing balls, violet or rose petal conserves and freckle-removing cream. Among his more exotic pick-me-ups is a drink made with crushed pearls, coral and gold leaf, mixed with ambergris and musk as well as sugar, dried fruit and herbs – it must have been like drinking perfume. He's not alone by any means. Elizabethan literature is full of similar eccentricities.

Tobacco was used as a medicinal herb by Native Americans, who taught the Spanish all about it, but when seeds were sent back home to Spain the plants were originally grown as ornamental garden flowers. Tobacco's alternative uses came to light only later, and soon it was being used medicinally throughout Europe, as a universal cure-all. Little did we know...

Tomatoes were discovered by early Spanish colonists; the 'tomatl' was a weed growing in Mexican fields, the plant having escaped from its original home in the South American Andes by hitching a ride down the ancient Aztec drainage canals. The Spaniards sent seeds home in 1550, and the plants were grown for their curious fruit. From Spain, tomatoes quickly spread around southern Europe, becoming popular in Italy, where they were colloquially known as *pomo di mori* (Moor's apple) – they came there from Moorish Spain. From Italy they spread to France as *pomme d'amour*, so by the time they reached England, tomatoes were known as 'love apples'.

The Elizabethan fascination with aphrodisiacs, coupled with the fruit's suggestive name, gave tomatoes a certain notoriety that lasted for the best part of 250 years, and for a long time tomatoes were grown only as rather risqué decorative plants.

Coconuts were introduced by Francis Drake who, in the *Golden Hind*, was the first man to sail around the world. On a stop-over in the tropics his men collected coconuts to eke out their rations, so Drake brought some back to England and presented one to the Queen who, by all accounts, was very pleased with it. Thanks to his exotic cargo, which also included

cloves from the Spice Islands and other trade goods, Drake's voyage made a small fortune for the private investors who funded his trip.

ELIZABETHANS AT PLAY

Bowling had already appeared as a pub game as early as the fourteenth century, and the occasional castle with room to spare had a bowls pitch, usually with a hard surface.

Henry VIII had grass bowling greens at Hampton Court, as his father had before him at Richmond Palace, but it wasn't until Elizabeth's time that bowls really rose to fame and a bowling green became an essential ingredient of fashionable gardens.

England and Spain were the rival superpowers of their day, and constantly at daggers drawn. Finally, the Spanish cracked, and on 20 May 1588 sent their Armada – the largest fleet ever mustered – to invade England. The English had an idea what was coming and had already organized a series of beacons along the south coast that needed only to be lit to warn of the Armada's approach – a bonfire was the quickest available means of communication at the time.

When the warning came, Sir Francis Drake was enjoying a quiet game of bowls on Plymouth Hoe, and is reputed to have said 'Let them wait their turn' as he finished his game. We don't know who won the game, but he sent the Spanish packing.

It's sometimes suggested that Drake played bowls on a chamomile lawn rather than grass, but I think it unlikely. You can't cut chamomile anything like as short as grass, so the bowls would not have run evenly over its surface.

Why call them tulips?

Busbecq, the diplomat who sent the Flemish botanist Clusius his first tulips, thought the flowers looked like the local headgear in Turkey, the part of the world they came from, so he described them as tulband, *the Dutch for 'turban'. By the time they reached England, this became mispronounced as 'tulipam', which was later shortened to 'tulip'.*

For the first time, lawns were being grown from grass alone – without the wild flowers of the medieval flowery mead – but cutting could still only be done with scythes, and a smooth, firm, well-beaten playing surface was becoming more necessary than ever.

Tulip Fever

As a result of the merchant adventurers' voyages to far-flung places, plant introductions were happening all over Europe. Bulbs were soon to be the next big thing in England, the craze having already started in Holland. Charles de l'Ecluse (1526–1609), who worked under the Latinized name of Carolus Clusius, was the father of the Dutch bulb trade.

Born in what is now southern Holland, he became an eminent scholar and botanist who regularly corresponded with all the great gardeners of his day, and made plant-collecting trips throughout Europe and the Ottoman Empire.

From 1573 to 1587 he was director of the imperial gardens in Vienna, and it was whilst working there that he received a parcel of tulip bulbs from a diplomat in Constantinople named Busbecq. In 1587 Clusius returned home to Holland to become director of a new botanical and horticultural study centre, taking some tulips with him. He went on to mastermind the introduction of tulips, crown imperials and other flower bulbs.

In 1593 Clusius became professor of botany at Leiden University where he started a botanic garden especially for the cultivation of all the new plant introductions, and wrote *Rariorum Plantarum Historia* (1601), a botanical classic on rare plants.

Of all the bulbs Clusius introduced, tulips were to cause the most trouble. In the seventeenth century an outbreak of a virus (tulip fire) infected large numbers of bulbs, causing bizarrely streaked, striped, flamed and other wildly variegated flowers to appear. These proved irresistible to collectors, causing a 'run' on rare varieties that was to become a horticultural South Sea Bubble. Being an altruistic scientist, Clusius refused to allow the trade access to his bulbs. As a result, his gardens were raided and the bulbs stolen.

Individual bulbs would change hands for enormous sums of money. When 'Tulipomania' reached its peak, single bulbs of choice varieties would sell for as much as 10,000 guilders each – the price of a fashionable house in the middle of Amsterdam. Things never went that mad in England, but tulips were sought after as show-off flowers in upper-crust gardens long after the 'bubble' burst in Holland and prices crashed. That happened in 1637, when a decree was passed stating that all traders must now honour their promissory notes. They could not, and thousands of people across Europe faced ruin. In Holland this extended to government coffers and resulted in the army and navy being drastically reduced. This in turn made it difficult for the country to defend its new colonies. As a result, New Amsterdam in America was captured by the English and renamed New York. All because of a tulip.

Blowsy, stripy tulips were a favourite subject for the seventeenth-century Dutch flower painters, so although the old varieties don't exist now you can still see what they were like. The closest thing we have today, the antique-look 'Rembrandt' tulip, is the result of breeding, not virus infection.

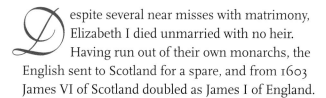

James I to William and Mary (1603–1702)

RENAISSANCE, REPRESSION AND RESTORATION

THE HOUSE OF STUART

James I 1603–25

Charles I 1625–48

Charles II 1660–85

James II 1685–89

William III and Mary II
   jointly 1689–94

William III alone 1694–1702

Anne 1702–14

Despite several near misses with matrimony, Elizabeth I died unmarried with no heir. Having run out of their own monarchs, the English sent to Scotland for a spare, and from 1603 James VI of Scotland doubled as James I of England.

KING JAMES

Within a couple of years of coming to the throne, the very horticulturally aware King James, had raised gardening to the status of a 'proper' profession, establishing the Gardeners Company of the City of London by royal charter. It was a gardening group with teeth. Under the terms of the charter nobody was allowed to practise gardening within six miles of the city without the company's say-so, and members were also entitled to destroy any plants, seeds and bulbs on sale in any markets on 'their patch' that didn't come up to scratch.

James knew a good garden when he saw it, and one that particularly took his fancy was Theobalds at Cheshunt, the home of Sir Robert Cecil, Earl of Salisbury, whose father Lord Burleigh had entertained Elizabeth I so handsomely. The house not only had one of the best gardens in the country, it also had a large deer park – and next to gardening, James's favourite hobbies were hunting and falconry. You can already hear the alarm bells ringing.

With a bit of regal string-pulling in 1607, James persuaded Sir Robert to swap his country house for an unwanted old royal palace – Hatfield House in Hertfordshire. The best thing going for Hatfield was a bit of history. It had been built in 1490 as a bishop's palace, then 'acquired' for the Crown by Henry VIII

(yes, the old story) and used as one of his many family homes. (It was while reading under an oak tree in the garden at Hatfield that his daughter Elizabeth received the news that she was finally to be made queen). Other than that, it was a wreck.

Theobalds was to become James's favourite palace. He planted mulberries in the garden, having been very impressed by the enormous amounts of money the French earned from their home-grown silk industry, and thought something similar would make a nice little earner. It sounded like a dead cert. You only needed silkworms and some mulberry leaves to feed them on, then you just sat back and waited for the cash to roll in.

He had over 1,000 mulberry trees planted at various sites, and persuaded many of his courtiers to try a few trees at their country estates. He head-hunted Robert Cecil's gardener, Mountain Jenings, to take charge of the mulberries at Theobalds, and in London he established a four-acre mulberry plantation in the king's hunting park, on part of the ground now occupied by Buckingham Palace.

The mulberry trees thrived, but there was one small problem – James's silkworm 'expert' was no horticulturist, so he'd recommended the wrong sort of mulberries. Instead of the white mulberries silkworms eat, James planted black mulberries (left), the fruiting sort. The result – a complete flop. James lost thousands of pounds on the venture.

OPPOSITE ABOVE: At the end of the Tudor reign foreign styles, notably that of the Dutch Het Loo garden, brought over by William III, continued to influence English garden design.

OPPOSITE BELOW: Parterres such as this one at Manor Hall, Bledlow, became popular successors to the Tudor knot garden.

RENAISSANCE, REPRESSION AND RESTORATION

Hatfield House in High Fashion

Even though he probably wasn't wild about the deal at the time, Robert Cecil seems to have given Hatfield House his best shot. He rebuilt it, retaining only the Tudor Great Hall (the house you see there now is his), and started making a new garden. To be sure, it was all done in the very latest horticultural fashion: he used teams of garden constructors imported specially from France, where a new Francophile form of Italian Renaissance gardening was taking off.

They put in a new terrace at the back of the house with steps leading down to the garden, where the main attraction was to be a highly ambitious Renaissance-style water feature. The centrepiece of this was a huge marble basin with a classical statue, from which water flowed through a shell-studded rivulet to an ornamental lake with an island in the middle. The whole thing was very fancy, and it's even claimed that fake fish 'swam' in the water – real ones brought all sorts of problems.

The trouble was, it needed some rather fancy hydraulics to run it, and Cecil's original engineer made a complete hash of the job. He was sacked and a Frenchman, Salomon de Caux, was brought in. He had to start again completely from scratch but, even so, the waterworks always played up.

The Tradescants

However, the Hatfield House story brings John Tradescant into horticultural history. He was working at Hatfield at the time of Cecil's takeover, and between him and Salomon de Caux the gardens took shape.

The Frenchman was an engineer who'd studied in Italy and had 'absorbed' Renaissance garden style while there. He was taken on by James's queen, Anne of Denmark, in 1607 to give some of the royal gardens a new look. He 'did' Greenwich and Richmond palaces, and also 'tweaked' Somerset House for the Prince of Wales. He's thought to be responsible for the first threads of Renaissance style creeping into royal gardens. That influence grew under the guidance of his close relative Isaac de Caux, who went on to work for James's successor, Charles I.

So when Robert Cecil took over Hatfield House he employed John Tradescant (1570–1638) as gardener/botanist to lay out the grounds, which

involved Tradescant travelling to all the big horticultural centres of Europe to find 'strange and rare' plants for his boss.

After leaving Cecil's employ, Tradescant took on other gardening jobs, but he still had the plant-hunting bug. He went on various perilous expeditions, including one to Algiers from which he brought back a golden Barbary apricot he'd set his heart on growing, and a trade mission sent by James I to Russia from which he returned with lots of new plants.

He finally settled in Lambeth, London, where his rapidly growing plant collection filled the garden. He set aside a room in his house as a museum (the first in Britain) for souvenirs of his travels. A compulsive collector, he acquired everything and anything – stuffed animals, lizards, fish and birds (including a dodo from Mauritius), ethnic footwear and clothing, carved cherry stones, lumps of rock... Mrs Trad must have been well pleased. At the end of his life he was working as gardener at Oatlands in Surrey, one of Henry VIII's old hunting lodges which was by then owned by Charles I.

John Tradescant the younger (1608–62) followed in his father's footsteps. He worked as his assistant for some years and became a plant-hunter; his introductions include the tulip tree, the swamp cypress, Virginia creeper, phlox, lupins, golden rod

Skirrets

Skirrets (Sisum sisarum) were popular root vegetables throughout the sixteenth and seventeenth centuries, but have rarely been heard of since. Charles I's cook had a recipe for skirret pie, made with boiled skirrets, chestnuts and slices of hard-boiled eggs in a butter and lemon sauce, flavoured with cinnamon and nutmeg, then – presumably – baked in a pastry 'coffin' (historical chefs were notoriously slack about detail). As for oven temperatures and timings, forget it. You simply played it by ear.

and Michaelmas daisies. His main stamping-ground was the British colony of Virginia in the USA, where he was working in 1638 when news reached him of his father's death. He immediately returned to England to take over his dad's royal gardening job, before moving home to run the Lambeth garden and the Ark.

The Tradescants were buried in the churchyard at St Mary-at-Lambeth in Lambeth Palace Road, which now houses the Museum of Garden History. Strangely enough, the contents of Tradescant's Ark are not in the museum. They passed to the antiquary Elias Ashmole in somewhat dubious circumstances – gambling debts and disputed wills come into it – and became the basis of the Ashmolean Museum in Oxford. The Lambeth garden has long since gone. The Tradescants were, however, the first of the professional plant-hunters, and the rate of new introductions steps up steeply from now on.

GARDENING UNDER THE PURITANS

James I was succeeded by Charles I, who extended the grounds at Richmond Palace by enclosing 2,500 acres of land and stocking them with two species of deer to make Richmond Park. He also took on Isaac de Caux to continue injecting gentle doses of Continental ideas into the Jacobean gardens he'd inherited. His French queen, Henrietta Maria, shared his enthusiasm and promptly called in a French gardener, André Mollet, to lay out fashionable new gardens at Somerset House and at her manor house in Wimbledon.

But just as everything in the garden was looking rosy, along came the English Civil War to throw a spanner in the works. Oliver Cromwell took over and he not only executed King Charles in 1649, but also confiscated the royal palaces and trashed the royal gardens. Anything of a remotely frivolous nature was right out as far as the Puritans were concerned: the only kind of gardening they approved of was vegetable-growing, but new introductions, such as potatoes, were off-limits because they weren't mentioned in the Bible.

Windsor Castle was turned into a prison for captured Royalists, and the Great Park was divided up into small, affordable parcels of land and sold off. Cromwell totally demolished Oatlands, Theobalds and Henrietta Maria's house at Wimbledon, and sold a lot of other royal residences. But he hung on to Whitehall Palace and Hampton Court, and moved his family in.

Nobody was allowed to sit on the fence during the Civil War. You either had to side with Cromwell's Roundheads, or – like most of the gardening and botany fraternity – with the pro-Royalist cavaliers. A lot of wealthy families sensibly took themselves off-side. Some holed up at their country houses for the duration, and others felt they'd be a lot safer moving to the Continent, where they spent their time catching up on all the latest gardening developments. As it turns out, that was quite a good move.

CONTINENTAL INFLUENCES

While English gardens had been stuck in something of a design time-warp – they were still based on the medieval square-grid layout – things

were really sizzling across the Channel. In France gardening had taken the Italian Renaissance look on board in a big way, adapted it to suit itself and really leapt ahead.

The baroque gardens of the *grand siècle* (golden age) were designed to be walked through following a predetermined route so that you saw all the different features in the right order, with vistas alternating with 'surprises'.

First, close to the house, were *parterres de broderie*. These were next-generation knot gardens, made from dwarf, clipped evergreens planted to re-create the intricate scrolls and flounces of embroidery patterns. Like knot gardens, they were surfaced with different coloured sands and meant to be seen from above.

Then you came to *parterres de gazon* – ornamental beds made from patterns cut into turf. These would be followed by *bosquets*, which were blocks of ornamental woodland divided up into formal sections

by wide, straight paths – *allées* or alleys – leading up to the vistas. Among the blocks of trees would be 'garden rooms' containing the 'surprises', which could be flower gardens, labyrinths or other features.

The gardens of the *grand siècle* were revolutionary compared to English ones, but when the Sun King, Louis XIV, threw money at it, the result was one of the most spectacular gardens ever – Versailles.

The brains behind it was André Le Nôtre. Born in France in 1613, Le Nôtre first worked as apprentice to his father, who was superintendent of the French royal gardens. His big break came when he worked at Vaux-le-Vicomte, a grand estate which, with his help, was fast becoming something special. The statesman owner, Jean Fouquet, made the mistake of inviting Louis XIV down for a visit to the opening. The Sun King was not amused to find that the place outshone his best garden, Fontainebleau, so, in a gesture typical of Henry VIII, he promptly had

ABOVE: This garden at Rousham, Oxfordshire, echoes the seventeenth-century fashion for planting parterres – *more elaborate relatives of the earlier knot gardens.*

RENAISSANCE, REPRESSION AND RESTORATION

Fouquet imprisoned and took Le Nôtre on as his own gardener. The result – Versailles. It was probably the most glamorous garden in the world at the time, and is still very impressive today despite inevitable economies.

Immediately next to the palace were the *parterres de broderie* which were, naturally, bigger and better than anyone else's. There was the orangery, the biggest ever built – 508ft long x 42ft wide x 45ft high – which housed 1,200 orange trees and several hundred other tender exotic plants that stood outside in summer. Out in the grounds were canals and elaborate fountains, and *bosquets* planted with semi-mature trees to give immediate effect. The whole thing made the perfect setting for the Sun King's extravagant costume balls, when thousands of guests descended on the gardens for torch-lit banquets, dancing and gondola trips down the canals.

Cut flowers to decorate the palace parties were grown in vast *parterres fleuriste,* or cutting gardens tucked away out of sight so that they wouldn't spoil the view.

Le Nôtre went on to design many other great gardens throughout Europe. His trademark was to create a major vista with gardens laid out geometrically on either side of it; and his Big Effect was achieved by introducing changes of level, which turned the garden into a natural theatre for his rich clients to show themselves off in – he didn't work for just anyone.

But even people who couldn't afford to commission Le Nôtre themselves saw his grand gardens and took away ideas to rehash back home. The seeds he sowed influenced all the smart gardens of his time. In Britain the emergent trend was to design the garden with the grand mansion as

OPPOSITE: *Versailles was the envy of the world, and its designer, André Le Nôtre, was much sought after by wealthy land-owners. It had a huge impact on other gardens across Europe.*

the hub of a wagon-wheel pattern of avenues, with the gaps in-between the 'spokes' filled with very ornate features, so the house was the centre of its own elaborate and very formal universe – a sort of British baroque.

FEATURES OF SEVENTEENTH-CENTURY GARDENS

The seventeenth century saw big changes in the style of grand gardens, but although the English had taken to Continental ways, and gardens were by now massive in scale, formality and complexity, they were still surrounded by hunting parks. By the second half of the century, plants were becoming an important part of gardens for the first time: enthusiasts were going for rare flowers, tender exotics and the means to keep them through winter, and trees, shrubs and evergreens were starting to feature. Striped – meaning variegated – hollies, were the up-and-coming thing.

ABOVE: Parterres were hugely popular and became extremely complex as gardeners sought to outdo one another. For those with big ideas but lacking inspiration, books with a variety of designs were available.

Parterres

Parterres were the big new gardening development of the seventeenth century. They were basically level areas containing ornamental flowerbeds, usually in complicated patterns, created close to the house where they could be looked down on from above, and separated from the rest of the garden by hedges or stone balustrades. The outlines of the design were picked out in tightly clipped box so that the effect was maintained all year round, since there wasn't much in the way of bedding plants at the

time. Parterres originated in France and first appeared in England in 1639. By 1664 they had completely taken over from knot gardens at fashionable houses.

Parterres de broderie

These were a much more ornate form of flowerbed, and were literally 'embroidery on the ground' – incredibly intricate designs that duplicated the scrolls and flounces of embroidery patterns. The idea was pioneered by André Mollet, who first

gardened for Charles I's queen, Henrietta Maria, and later for Charles II.

Fountains

Incredibly elaborate fountains were the order of the day and needed advanced hydraulics. At Chatsworth, laid out between 1687 and 1706 by London & Wise (see page 93), there were some of the most spectacular and technically advanced fountains of the time. The copper willow tree, the 'leaves' of which continuously dripped water as if after rain,

and the Grand Cascade, (laid out by a pupil of Le Nôtre's in 1694) 'producing a thunderous roar like the Egyptian cataracts', are still there today.

Wildernesses

These were add-ons intended to enlarge the garden. They weren't wild gardens, but formal pleasure grounds enclosed by tall hedges and planted with groves of trees, divided by hedges and grass paths into 'garden rooms' which might contain a *parterre*, an arbour and seat, or scented shrubs.

ABOVE: The Grand Cascade at Chatsworth, Derbyshire, is a spectacular sight and a testament to the skill of the garden technicians of the seventeenth century.

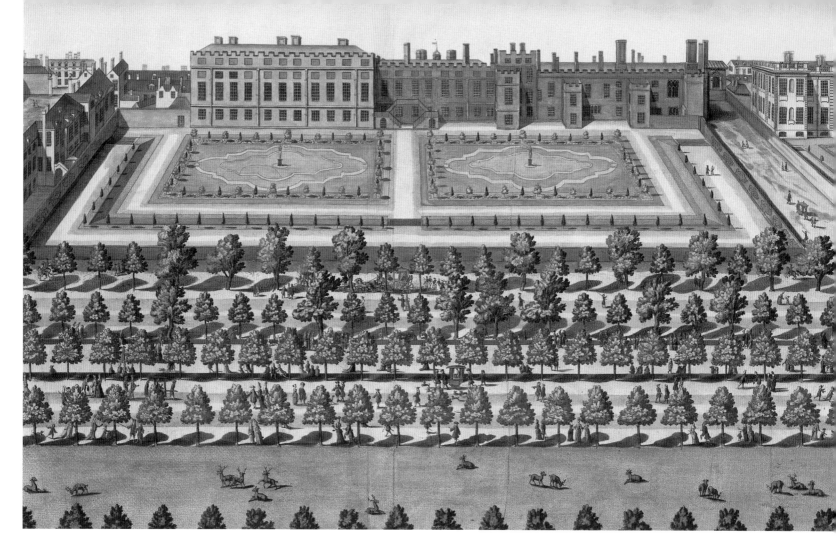

Bananas

The first bananas ever seen in London were displayed in the window of Thomas Johnson, an apothecary, on 10 April 1633. When, in June, the fruit were found to have turned soft, they were sliced up and sampled. The verdict? 'A pleasant taste, soft and tender.' We now each eat an average of 11lb of bananas every year.

Enthusiasts' Plants and Tender Exotics

The second half of the seventeenth century saw a big rise in the number of exotic and tender plants arriving in Britain from all over the world, which quickly became collectors' pieces. Enthusiasts kept a separate enclosed area for their 'treasures', which might be covered with bell jars for protection when necessary, and might also have a winter-house for sheltering oranges and other tender 'greens'. This was a garden building with large south-facing glass windows which would be closed on cold nights and, if necessary, covered with mats for insulation. By 1690 there were more greenhouses and conservatories about, but, being new, people didn't have much of a clue how to look after the plants growing in them. Some of the grandest were heated with stoves, but normally pans of hot coals would be taken inside on cold nights. Orangeries were increasingly used as summer-houses for entertaining in when the plants were stood outside: they were only moved under cover in winter.

THE RETURN OF ROYALTY AND GARDENING

It wasn't just travelling nobles who were impressed by Continental gardens. When the Civil War started, Charles I's twelve-year-old heir had fled abroad for safety. He spent years in exile, travelling in Holland and France, and spent a lot of time at Versailles. The net result was that by the time the war ended and the monarchy was restored in 1660 the 30-year-old Charles II had acquired a great taste for the French royal gardening style.

On returning home Charles badly needed to make a splash to show the world that the British monarchy was back in business, big time. He decided that the best way to do so was by going on the gardening bender of a lifetime. The royal gardens that were left were, in any case, ripe for a makeover, seeing the state Cromwell's mob had left them in.

The style Charles plumped for was naturally the art-triumphing-over-nature look that he'd been surrounded by for the previous few years. It was sufficiently glamorous to provide him with a

suitably spectacular platform from which to make his mark. But first he had to find the right gardener for the job.

As a fan of André Le Nôtre's work, Charles tried to tempt him to England to lay out some of the royal gardens – particularly St James's Park in London which he saw as his big showpiece. But, though the French king gave permission for the loan of his star garden designer, Le Nôtre didn't come

Next, Charles tried to poach Louis XIV's head gardener at Versailles, la Quintinie, but again failed – at which point he remembered the gardener his mother had used at Wimbledon, and appointed André Mollet as head gardener of St James's Park, with a team of French gardeners. Their brief was to give it the stylish new look.

Charles II's grandfather was Henri IV of France, who'd created some fairly spectacular gardens of his own, with the help of his gardener Claude Mollet, who died in 1649. Mollet's sons, André and Claude (junior) travelled around Europe making gardens before moving to England. Their speciality was French-style gardens with elaborate *parterres* and canals lined with avenues of trees, like the one at Fontainebleau. But what made them stand out from other top-notch garden planners is that instead of relying heavily on architecture, they worked with plants. Their trademark was the *parterre de broderie* – a series of intricate, embroidery-like patterns made of closely clipped box set against variously coloured backgrounds, first thought up by their father. *Parterre de broderie* quickly became the Next Big Thing, pushing knot gardens right out of fashion.

When work began at St James's Park in 1661, it was still much as it had been since Henry VIII

bought it – a royal hunting park in-between St James's Palace and Whitehall. Under Mollet's guidance a huge canal – 2,800ft long and 100ft wide – was built through the middle, with the gardens arranged on either side so that each was a mirror image of the other. Charles walked his spaniels through the formal avenues of trees bordering the water; a menagerie and duck ponds were put in, and aviaries full of exotic birds were installed along what is now known as Birdcage Walk. Today's Pall Mall takes its name from the *paille-maille* courts Charles had put in so he could play the fashionable French game, which was something like croquet.

Immediately next to the palace were turf *parterres* surrounded by geometric *bosquets* of ornamental trees and shrubs planted round a large, old oak tree, which was left as a touch of royal 'déjà vu'.

Although royal gardens were usually kept strictly for use by the royal family and their guests, things were different in St James's Park – the public were allowed in. The King was keen to meet the people, and was often out alone, walking his dogs and chatting with passers-by, which seems incredible when you think of the security that goes with any kind of royal outing nowadays.

When Mollet died in 1666 Charles needed a new gardener for St James's Park, and appointed John Rose. He had the right background to continue the work, having studied under Le Nôtre at Versailles, but his great claim to fame is that he's supposed to have grown the first pineapple ever ripened in Britain. The story stems from a portrait in which he's shown presenting one to the King, but I'm inclined to think a certain amount of artistic licence crept in and it was actually a curiosity brought back from abroad.

OPPOSITE: St James's Park was always intended to be a Royal showpiece and, when finished, Charles II shared it with the public, allowing them to walk around it as he and his family did.

Quinine

Cinchona trees grow wild in the South American Andes, where the local Indians, who were well versed in herbal medicine, used the bark to treat fevers.

The powdered bark contains quinine, the first effective remedy for malaria, and because it was first brought to Europe by Jesuit priests it became known as 'Jesuits' powder'. At the time, malaria wasn't just a tropical disease; it also occurred in England. Charles II caught malaria and successfully took the cure, but Oliver Cromwell wouldn't touch what he thought of as 'powder of the devil' because of its Catholic connections, and died of the disease. So it was that a mere mosquito altered the course of British history.

Charles's Gardens

Charles II decided to do up the Palace of Whitehall and use it for his parliament. It was a bit of a wreck as nothing much had been done to it since Henry VIII's day, apart from the new Banqueting Hall in the garden, designed by Inigo Jones for Charles I (who was executed there). So the old palace was given a brand-new façade and a fashionable garden complete with canal. Charles also ordered a highly decorated, state-of-the-art sundial, which was a great status symbol at the time, for the garden. His father had been known to carry a pocket model around with him, but Charles II's Whitehall wonder didn't just tell the time – it also gave all sorts of amazing astronomical and astrological information, and was, by all accounts, quite a talking point.

Windsor Castle had been badly damaged by the Roundheads (who'd also sold off the Great Park), and it needed a lot of improvements to bring it back up to scratch. Charles brought in Hugh May to make a palatial baroque garden, with the castle at its heart and avenues radiating out all round like the spokes of a wheel. Work began in 1680 and was still going on years later. In 1689 Charles bought back most of the bits of land that made up Windsor Great Park, and planted the Long Walk – a two-and-a-half-mile avenue of elm trees linking the park to the castle.

One thing King Charles needed to give the newly restored monarchy street cred was a queen, so early in his reign the King of Portugal's daughter, Catherine of Braganza, was chosen, and Hampton Court was given a new look in preparation for the wedding in 1662. Mollet was brought in to restyle

the gardens along similar lines to St James's Park. His main thrust revolved round the view from the queen's bedroom window. A new balcony was built from which she'd look straight down the new, mile-long canal, dug to line up with it, with the gardens arranged symmetrically on either side.

But after the marriage Catherine was hardly ever there to enjoy the view. The union with Charles was a typical royal marriage of convenience, and the Queen was almost immediately sidelined. She spent most of her life at Somerset House (where Charles's mother had made a new garden just before the Civil War), while the King kept a string of mistresses. Meanwhile, all that effort at Hampton Court didn't go to waste – it made an impressive base for Charles to entertain official visitors.

One of the many royal houses that Cromwell knocked about a bit was Greenwich, but rather than restore it Charles decided to replace it with a brand-new palace. The old one was pulled down in readiness, and Charles envisaged some grand gardens that would be quite different from anything that had gone before.

He wanted André Le Nôtre to supervise the work, and Louis XIV had agreed to loan him out specially, but, as was the case with St James's Park, it was not to be. Le Nôtre did, however, send some plans. They show that the steep hillside of the site was to be terraced, with cascades flowing down the giant 'steps', and a huge *parterre* surrounded by raised walkways from which visitors to the garden would look down on to the elaborate embroidery-pattern planting within – something like a gigantic sunken garden.

They made a start, and £2,000 was spent on earth-moving, but only a small part of the planned palace was ever built (it's still there today, only now it's the Royal Naval College) and, though the gardens were quite well advanced, they were never finished. Charles finally abandoned the project in 1674.

Once the new baroque garden style gained ground at royal level all the major nobles immediately started altering their own gardens to keep up to date. Knot gardens were out and *parterres de broderie* were very definitely in.

Restyling a grand garden cost a fortune, and not just because of the manpower and hardware involved; plants were becoming a major item of expense as well. By now rare and expensive new shrubs and trees were the things to have, and towards the end of Charles's reign evergreens were just starting to come into fashion.

A lot of extravagant planting was done but, because gardens had always been architectural rather than horticultural, people didn't have well-honed cultivation skills. A lot of the new plant novelties died off. The old Tudor favourites had been no problem because they were mostly tough customers, which virtually looked after themselves. Now that gardens were going 'green', gardening books that gave practical advice on plant care suddenly became a must.

Chelsea Physic Garden

During James I's reign, back in 1617, a splinter group had broken away from the Grocers' Company and set itself up as the Apothecaries' Society. It wasn't till 1673 that it found itself a garden in which to grow 'simples' – medicinal herbs. For £5 a year, it leased from the future Lord Cheyne three acres of

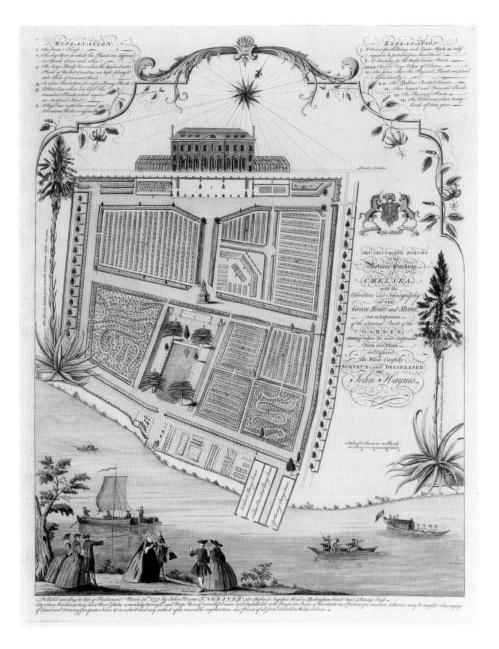

land in Chelsea, close to the site where Sir Christopher Wren later built the Royal Military Hospital, in whose grounds the Chelsea Flower Show is now staged every year.

A walled garden was created, and gradually the society gained a reputation for acquiring rare new plants from abroad, as well as simples – one of the earliest greenhouses was built with underfloor heating to house tender exotics. Chelsea Physic Garden was to prove a hotbed of great gardeners for centuries into the future.

In 1685 John Evelyn went to see the Apothecaries' Garden of Simples at Chelsea, as it was then called, where he saw – in the greenhouse – the cinchona

ABOVE: *The Chelsea Physic Garden in London was set up by the Apothecaries' Society in order to grow medicinal herbs and tender exotics in its glasshouses – work that continues there today.*

OPPOSITE AND OVERLEAF:
Het Loo in Holland was
home to William and Mary
before they inherited the
British throne, and
inevitably its grand garden
inspired those of their British
royal palaces.

JOHN EVELYN 1620–1706

ABOVE: *John Evelyn started
out as a scientist but became
a prolific gardening writer
and designer.*

Following his student days at Oxford University, John Evelyn studied chemistry and medicine in Europe, where he visited all the important gardens. Returning home, he redesigned his own 100-acre garden in Kent on Continental lines, put in a laboratory and nursery to satisfy his scientific instincts, and settled down to life as a gardening writer and designer. He was friends with the diarist Samuel Pepys, and a founder member of the Royal Society (whose aim was the advancement of science), which was given its royal charter by Charles II in 1662.

In 1664 Evelyn published a gardener's almanac, with month-by-month advice on which jobs were to be done but, unlike its modern equivalents, his version also gave the times of sunrise and sunset, and the number of hours of daylight – presumably so the gardeners knew how much time they had to get through all the work.

One of his major works, *Sylva, or a Discourse of Forest Trees*, was also published in 1664. Besides promoting tree-planting in general, Evelyn gives advice on transplanting large trees for readers re-creating fashionable, large-scale planting schemes. Basically, he says dig a trench round the tree in winter, insert wooden blocks under the root ball and fill the hole with water. Allow a hard frost to freeze it into a solid block, then lift it out with block and tackle. (Britain was in the grip of the Little Ice Age then.)

Within his 50 or so riveting books, Evelyn mentions all sorts of exotic-sounding garden accessories, such as hortulan architecture, piscinas, jettos, cryptae, gazon-theatres, artificial echoes, automata and hydraulic music. And I'm sure he invented his own words to baffle the uninitiated. What do you make, for instance, of 'ablaqueation' and 'stercoration'?

tree, the bark of which was to revolutionize medicine by providing a cure for malaria.

Almost a century later the land of the manor of Chelsea was bought by Sir Hans Sloane, who handed the physic garden over to the Apothecaries' Society in perpetuity in return for a payment of £5 per year.

The names Hans, Sloane and Cheyne are now all commemorated in street names, squares and walks around the area used by visitors to the Chelsea Flower Show and to the Chelsea Physic Garden, which opens especially throughout show week. The nearby King's Road in Chelsea was built specially for Charles II as a short cut from Whitehall to Hampton Court, by-passing the village of Knightsbridge, which was evidently a bit rough.

ROYAL ENTHUSIASTS

The end of the reign of Charles II's successor, James II, was followed by inevitable problems over the succession, and finally the Dutch Prince William of Orange came to the throne. He was married to Mary, who technically had a slightly stronger claim to the hot seat than he had, so in the interests of marital – not to say national – harmony the pair ruled jointly.

The great thing about having not one but two gardening-mad monarchs on the throne is that they brought twice the oomph to bear on the royal gardens. Their horticultural habit had got off to a head start as, before inheriting the British throne, the happy couple were already living at Het Loo in Holland, which had superb gardens. These had been laid out in 1680 as an adapted version of the grand French style, designed to suit the lie of the land.

Dutch baroque was strong on water features – being a low-lying country, Holland was already well awash – and canals were something the Dutch really understood. As the land was also very flat, Het Loo was perfect for laying out enormous *parterres*, so William and Mary really went to town on creating complicated shapes. But the Dutch avoided using lots of large trees, which were a major feature in gardens such as Versailles, because the high water-table killed off the roots before they could reach any appreciable size. Instead they went overboard on heavily clipped evergreen shrubs which, being shallow rooted, grew well.

Typically of baroque design everything at Het Loo was very symmetrical, arranged on each side of a central axis. The garden was full of *parterres* and wide walks decorated with classical statues, rills and elaborate fountains. All around the grounds stood potted orange trees, which were William's family emblem. In winter they were put away in an orangery along with other tender trees, such as oleander and pomegranate. As a keen horticulturist Mary built up quite a collection of rare plants, which was a tremendous status symbol at the time.

Around the edge of the garden was a new and very Dutch innovation – *plate bande*. These were narrow borders with indented shapes edged with box, especially designed to act as theatrical 'sets' in which to show off rare flowers. Instead of being planted thickly, the way you think of a border nowadays, collectors' pieces, such as tulips, would be well spaced out with bare soil in-between to make a style that's best described as more botanical print than chocolate-box lid. About the only garden where you'll see an authentic example of this is at Westbury Court, near Gloucester.

A New Dawn of Plant Use

Medical Matters

Medicine was very much in its early stages, and 'bleeding' was recommended for all sorts of problems. This procedure was carried out by barbers, who doubled as surgeons because they were dab hands with a cut-throat razor. The spiral red and white stripes of the barber's pole that was their shop sign represented blood and bandages, for the benefit of customers who could not read.

The 'King's Evil' – scrofula, a form of tuberculosis – was thought by some medical men to be cured by 'the touch of the sovereign', and Charles occasionally had to perform this unenviable task. Under Charles II, and with the help of organizations such as the Royal Society, medicine and surgery began to develop into more of a science.

Time for Tea

In the early 1660s the East India Company started importing small quantities of the leaves of an oriental evergreen shrub, *Camellia sinensis* (above), from China. Depending on which part of China it came from, it was called tay (Amoy), or ch'a (Canton). For the first time in history we could sit down to a nice cup of tea, and Samuel Pepys was one of the first people in England to try the new beverage – on 25 September 1661. His diary records: 'I sent for a cup of tea; a China drink, of which I had never drunk before.' What he thought of it he didn't say.

It can't have been cheap, though; the first consignments of tea leaves sold for £10 per pound. With admirable PR savvy, the East India Company presented two pounds of it to Charles II, and his queen, Catherine, gave tea the royal seal of approval by encouraging it at court. The Company promptly began importing cups or bowls and other tea-related paraphernalia from China, which turned the drink into a fashionable afternoon ritual, and tea drinking took off.

The government then began to tax tea, which raised £3 million a year – enough to pay half the running costs of the navy. Cheaper tea could be obtained by smuggling it in from the Continent, but by the eighteenth century there was also a thriving trade in 'smoach' – counterfeit tea made by mixing genuine China tea with dried and curled hawthorn-tree leaves.

Only the very rich made tea at home. To start with, it was mostly sold ready to drink in coffee houses. These were all-male preserves and tea houses were for ladies – the first one was opened by Thomas Twining in London in 1717. In 1732 the Vauxhall Pleasure Gardens opened as a tea garden where both genders could meet to drink tea, chat and enjoy open-air concerts without creating a scandal. Vauxhall Gardens are still with us, though rather less pleasure is taken there today.

Culinary Interlude

Salads, or sallets as they were first known, became fashionable food in the seventeenth century, and a huge range of extraordinary greengrocery was used in them. James II's gardener was once quoted as saying that a good sallet should have at least 35 ingredients, and garden writer to the gentry John Evelyn brought out the ultimate salad book, *Acetaria, a Discourse on Sallets*, in 1699. He felt that a good sallet should be composed like music, with all the ingredients falling into place like the notes. The ingredients included:

- Salad greens – young leaves of primrose, cowslip, rocket, violet, sow thistle, tansy, marigold, jack by the hedge, lettuce, cresses, samphire, yarrow, scurvy grass, leek tips, young spinach, succory (wild chicory), stonecrop, wood sorrel, nasturtium, nettle tips, dandelion.
- Flower buds (often preserved for winter by being stored in vinegar or candied in sugar) – violet, cowslip, wild strawberry, gilliflower, primrose, rosemary, alexanders, elderflower.
- Roots – elecampane, daisy, rampion, radish, angelica, parsnip, carrot (often boiled or candied), skirret, viper-grass (salsify).
- Herbs – sage, tarragon, borage, hyssop.
- Various – ash keys, pickled broom, tendrils of hops, vine and peas, assorted wild fungi, earth nuts (the knobbly lumps on the roots of the pignut, *Conopodium majus*, a member of the cow parsley family.
- Dressing – 'oyle and best wine vinegar impregnated with the infusion of clove gillyflowers, elder roses, rosemary and nasturtium'.

The ingredients were to be prepared with a silver knife, and 'exquisitely cull'd and cleansed of all worm eaten, slimy, cankered, dry, spotty or any ways vitiated leaves'. Quite so.

Where to see authentic Dutch-style gardens today

Levens Hall, Cumbria
The famous topiary garden (right) is still pretty well as it was laid out in 1694 when it was owned by Colonel James Grahame, keeper of James II's Privy Purse. On James's abdication, the colonel diplomatically left court and retired to Levens, where he had the garden laid out between 1689 and 1712 by Guillaume Beaumont, a pupil of Le Nôtre, who had previously worked for James II at Hampton Court.

Hampton Court, Surrey
William III's huge, baroque privy garden has been recently restored to its original form, complete with authentic seventeenth-century plants. There are formal parts, a central, circular pool with a fountain, and many intricately patterned beds edged with dwarf clipped box. Yew pyramids give height, and a shady *allée* runs down one side. The is terminated with a semi-circle of ornate, wrought-iron panels by Tijou.

Westbury Court, near Gloucester
This rare seventeenth-century, Dutch-style water garden has canals, elaborate fountains, vistas and alleys, with borders authentically laid out to display enthusiasts' rare plants, and a collection of seventeenth-century plants. The house is no longer there, but the garden is remarkable.

Het Loo, Holland
The Prince of Orange's garden in Apeldoorn has been re-created as it was in 1684, and is said to be the very best example of its style, with elaborate water features, *parterres* and a sunken garden.

CENTURY OF CATASTROPHES

The seventeenth century must have been a trying time for gardeners, due to the unprecedented series of natural disasters that occurred.

Frost

The climate, which had been mild enough in medieval times for vast vineyards to be paying propositions, had been steadily deteriorating from roughly 1550 onwards. By the mid-seventeenth century the winters were very cold indeed, and would continue so until the early eighteenth century. A wide crust of ice formed on the sea round the coastline of Britain each winter, and the river Thames froze over 11 times, allowing Londoners to hold 'frost fairs' on the ice. The coldest winter was 1683–4, when the ice on the river was a foot thick and didn't melt for two months. All the cedars of Lebanon in the country died.

Climate change had its effect on summer weather, too. Some years were very cool, and the growing season could be up to five weeks shorter than usual. But some summers were hot and dry, and in 1665 it was so bad that the Thames virtually dried up.

Plague

Bubonic plague had been occurring on and off in Britain for 300 years, but a particularly severe outbreak hit London in 1665, and by the end of that year had killed over 70,000 locals.

The outbreak started in the Drury Lane area, just up the road from the home of Samuel Pepys. His diary entry for the day mentions seeing a red cross and the words 'Lord Have Mercy Upon Us' written on doors of affected houses. Pepys bought some tobacco, purely for medicinal purposes, then sent his wife away to the country for safety. He stayed in London himself, having a high old time. 'I have never lived so merrily,' he wrote.

Charles II holed up for a while at Syon House to avoid the plague – a successful strategy. But the disease hit the poor far more than the rich since – in London particularly – the poor lived in overcrowded, filthy and rat-infested houses where conditions were perfect for the plague to spread.

Physicians had no idea of its cause. People wore spice-filled face-masks and carried herbal nosegays in an attempt to ward off the plague. The only 'treatment' – a herbal remedy of buttercup roots and herbs infused in wine – was not the least bit effective.

Fire

On 2 September 1666 a spark from the bread-oven at a bakery in Pudding Lane set the shop on fire, and the flames soon spread to nearby warehouses, which – unluckily as it happens – were packed with pitch and other highly inflammable goods. It took five days to put out the Great Fire of London (above), and by then 100,000 people had lost their homes and St Paul's Cathedral had burnt down.

But by clearing out all the old, ramshackle wooden buildings and evicting the rats the fire loosened the grip of the plague, and the way was clear for London to be given a major new facelift, with Sir Christopher Wren in charge.

The Great Hurricane

To cap a century of catastrophes, in 1703 England was hit by a hurricane of roughly the same force as the one experienced in southern England in 1987. Winds of 120 m.p.h. felled trees and flattened houses all over the country, killing 8,000 people, and demolishing the new Eddistone lighthouse, which had only just been built.

When William and Mary succeeded to the English throne they continued to live in Holland for a time, and had Het Loo done up to suit their new status. They brought in the designer, Daniel Marot, who'd been trained by Le Nôtre, the creator of Versailles. His brief was to interior-decorate the house and give a new look to the *parterres* around it. Because he was doing both jobs, he was able to repeat the embroidery patterns he used on the fabrics indoors in the *parterres de broderie* in the garden, thus creating a coordinated house-and-garden look for perhaps the first time in recorded history – a trend that was soon to spread.

William and Mary's Des Res

When they moved to Britain William and Mary planned to spend as little time in London as possible, because the smoke and dust triggered off William's asthma attacks, but they nevertheless needed a base there. Since the Palace of Whitehall was damp, the couple bought Nottingham House in 1689. It was in the village of Kensington and came with 17 acres of garden, which they did up. Turf *parterres* were laid close to the house, leading out to a series of garden 'rooms' outlined with hedges and planted with trees, all arranged on either side of a central pathway leading out from the front of the house. Other than Hampton Court, it was to be the only garden William and Mary made in England, and when it was finished they changed the building's name to Kensington Palace. Unfortunately, nothing of their garden is left there today.

William and Mary decided to make Hampton Court, with its clean country air, their main home, and set about giving the gardens their biggest makeover ever.

Het Loo was used as the inspiration for the 'new look', as William wanted the garden to make him feel at home. Charles II's formal canal was a great help in that respect, so it stayed as the centrepiece of the new design.

ABOVE: Kensington Palace's garden was the only one in England that William and Mary finished; it displayed a bold use of Dutch-influenced turf parterres.

OVERLEAF: Preferring the country life, William and Mary turned their attentions from London to Hampton Court, which became their most ambitious project.

Sir Christopher Wren was given the job of creating a new classical-style façade for the east side of the palace; and to give Charles II's French-style garden a Dutch look they brought in Daniel Marot, who'd undertaken the improvements at Het Loo, along with a team of Dutch gardeners. At long last, Henry VIII's dated mount garden came down.

The royal couple took a great deal of personal interest in the work, with the help of a garden committee. In charge of this was the Earl of Portland (alias Hans Bentinck, who ran William's gardens in Holland), with George London as his deputy responsible for supervising the work.

BELOW: *The privy garden at Hampton Court was brought in line with current fashions by William and Mary, with a little help from a team of Dutch gardeners.*

George and his partner, Henry Wise, laid out Chatsworth and also ran a big nursery at Brompton Park, site of the Victoria and Albert Museum. The pair did some of the work for William and Mary at Kensington Palace, and would be royal gardeners for some time into the future.

Marot's Hampton Court

There weren't many English gardens where you could have got away with re-creating something in the Dutch baroque style, but luckily for Daniel Marot, enthused with the design, the land at Hampton Court was flat and, as it was right next to the Thames, there was plenty of water available.

Marot's first major project was the fountain garden, which he put up against the new Wren frontage on the east side of the palace. This was a huge, fan-shaped *parterre*, like the one at Het Loo, with a long, straight vista from the front of the house to a huge fountain in the middle, and on to Charles II's canal which already lined up with the centre of the house. Marot had to chop a bit off the end to fit in the fountain garden: its shortened form was known as the Long Water from then on.

The fan shape of the *parterre* itself was filled with a vast series of complicated *parterre de broderie* beds, planted in intricately scrolled patterns. The whole thing was dotted with statues and a further 11 fountains spaced regularly around the edge of the *parterre*, which you looked down on from a raised walk. Then the whole area was outlined with double rows of trees and wide avenues leading out in all directions across the surrounding park. It was deliciously extravagant.

While all this was going on, the Great Wilderness was being planted beyond the kitchen gardens, way out to the north of the house. A wilderness wasn't a wild garden in the least. At the time, the term was used to mean a formal enclosed area with paths running through it, and 'rooms' containing arbours, seats and shrubs outlined with hedges. Marot designed the Hampton Court wilderness in the shape of a huge rectangle divided by paths running from each corner and crossing in the middle, with lots of complicated sub-patterns fitted into the gaps to make a series of ornately shaped compartments, all outlined with hornbeam hedges. Within these compartments were various 'secret gardens', including a turf maze – the sort cut out of grass with gravel paths that you walk along – and the famous tall hedge maze, which is all that's left of the original wilderness today.

For the south side of the house Marot designed a new privy garden, with symmetrical baroque *parterres de broderie* planted in box picked out with coloured sands. The swirling scroll patterns were designed to match the interior decor of the house, as at Het Loo. But here, to make the gardens more interesting for visitors walking around instead of looking down from the windows, Marot left open soil in the centre of the *parterre* shapes so that they could be planted up with seasonal bedding. Not having real bedding plants, the gardeners used a backbone of standard-trained flowering shrubs, and set out a sequence of seasonal spring bulbs followed by perennial flowers grown in pots under glass.

Mary also had her own private flower garden at Hampton Court for her botanical collection, which she'd had sent over from Holland. Her more exotic 'greens' were parked at London & Wise's nursery every winter, where there were the facilities to care for them. Eventually, a glasshouse with underfloor heating, like the one at the Chelsea Physic Garden, was built for her at Hampton Court. The word 'greenhouse' comes from the original use of glass structures to house 'greens' – as rare, cold-tender – evergreens, such as oleander, were known at the time.

ABOVE: Hampton Court Palace was William and Mary's biggest and most dramatic makeover.

Turn in Fortunes

Everything was going according to plan but, in 1694, Mary died. William took her death very badly, and work on the gardens at Hampton Court came to a grinding halt. Nothing much happened for several years, until William had recovered enough to feel up to a new challenge. The Palace of Whitehall had burnt down in 1698, so he felt justified in blowing some money, as Hampton Court would have to take the strain of all that extra state entertaining. It was just as well – his next batch of improvements were to set him back £40,000.

Masses of sculptures were moved from St James's Park to give the fountain garden a facelift, and the privy garden was enlarged and given a massive makeover. Clipped hollies and yews were added, along with a large, single-jet fountain, scroll-patterned turf *parterres* and a banqueting house. Tubs of William's trademark orange trees were stood all around the gardens in summer. They were still quite a novelty in England at the time, but again they fast became quite the thing to grow once you had somewhere to house them, so orangeries came 'in' at the same time.

William continued to suffer badly from chest troubles. He clearly still missed Mary and began to hit the bottle. While he was riding in the park at Hampton Court one day, his horse tripped – put a foot down a mole hole, so it's thought – and as a result of his injuries William died several weeks later.

After William's death in 1702 Mary's sister, Anne, came to the throne. She'd never got on with either of them, and though she liked gardens she wasn't wild about William and Mary's *parterres* because she hated the smell of box. She didn't feel any warmer towards her deceased relatives when she saw the accounts – the gardens were costing a fortune. So, from a gardener's point of view, she behaved rather badly.

At Hampton Court Anne had all the *parterres* pulled out and replaced with a much simpler design of Dutch-style *plates bandes* (narrow borders with individual flowers well spaced out and lots of bare soil in-between them) as they cost much less to maintain. She also sent back some statues that William had ordered, which hadn't been paid for, and cleared his fountain garden away, all except for one single jet.

At Kensington Palace – which she was quite keen on – she splashed out on a £6,000 orangery, turned a natural hollow in the land into a sunken garden surrounded by 'viewing galleries', and pinched 30 acres of Hyde Park to turn them into a wilderness where she had ten ponds built.

Henry Wise was appointed as her head gardener, in charge of maintaining all the royal gardens, but she hacked the budget by two-thirds, to £1,600, which even in those days can't have been over-generous. However, for Henry it paid off. London & Wise, the firm in which he was a partner, became the smart garden maintenance firm for aspiring aristocrats from then on. As Anne's twelve-year reign moved on, clipped evergreens became the plants for smart gardens, and where did the top people go to buy them? Yes, the Brompton nursery of royal gardeners, London & Wise. But not for long. The gardening mood of the nation was ready for a sea change. The Dutch look turned out to be a mere flash in the pan.

ABOVE: William and Mary brought the Dutch style to British gardens and started a new fashion in design.

OPPOSITE: The privy garden at Hampton Court today – restored to its former late seventeenth-century glory.

Hampton Court costs

At the time of William's death there were 74 acres of royal gardens, with an annual maintenance budget of £4,800. Hampton Court swallowed half of this as the gardens were so elaborate. Labour was the largest single item of expense. The Earl of Portland received £200 as superintendent of the gardens, a weeding woman was paid 8d a day, and a mole-catcher cost £16 a year. Under the circumstances, William may well have felt like asking for his money back.

THE HOUSE OF HANOVER –
IMPROVING ON NATURE

THE HOUSE OF HANOVER

George I 1714–27

George II 1727–60

George III 1760–1820

George IV 1820–30

William IV 1830–37

OPPOSITE ABOVE: The Georgian era sparked a revolution in British gardening style and grand designs were de rigueur.

OPPOSITE BELOW: Gardens were becoming more reliant on landscaping, with the odd classical reference thrown in.

By the beginning of the Georgian era Britain had long since lost its natural landscape. Much of the native forest that covered England in the Stone Age was cut down by the Saxons to provide building materials and to clear the land for agriculture. What remained of its oak forest was felled for timber to make Tudor warships.

By the early eighteenth century, farming was the big earner. A quarter of the cultivated land was owned by just 400 families. But landowners didn't work – tenants and agricultural workers did that, leaving the owners free to devote their time to leisure. Fox-hunting was the new up-and-coming sport, so copses were specially planted. Landowners were also enclosing open countryside and making today's familiar patchwork pattern of fields. Some 200,000 miles of new hedging was planted round them; nurseries were coining it. Now that the countryside had been tamed, it was time for gardens to go wild.

Two things happened that turned the gardening world on its head during the Georgian era. After years of worsening relations with the French war finally broke out. Copying 'their' gardens now felt quite unpatriotic. After a century of decidedly man-made French-style formal gardens, gardeners were fed up with being influenced by 'them', and had had enough of geometric shapes, straight lines and tightly clipped evergreens. It was time for a change.

For some years, aristocrats had been sending their sons off abroad on a 'grand tour'. The idea was to broaden the mind, study foreign languages and soak up the culture. The young men learnt about life (wine, women, gambling...) but they also came home with a taste for wild scenery that was like nothing they'd ever seen at home – foaming waterfalls, snowcapped mountains with forested slopes and jagged, rocky crags.

Gardens were about to strike off in a completely new direction and, for once, Britain would lead Europe in gardening style. The scenic look came in.

REMARKABLE DEVELOPMENTS IN AN UNREMARKABLE REIGN

In 1714 complications over the royal succession brought a German prince to the throne. George, Elector of Hanover, wasn't all that keen on being George I. He didn't much like Britain, didn't speak the language and, worst of all, he wasn't interested in gardens or gardening.

His only redeeming feature was an interest in animals. He laid hands on 100 acres of Hyde Park near Kensington Palace to make a deer park, and part of it became a menagerie, which he filled with tigers and other big cats. He also had a large pond dug to keep turtles in, which is almost certainly the one we know today as Kensington Round Pond.

As gardening goes it was an unremarkable reign, apart from one thing – the first reliable instance of a home-grown pineapple appears, which started a great new aristocratic craze.

In 1720 Henry Telende, who was gardener to a modest baronet, used a hotbed to pull off this amazing feat. The hotbed was a brick-lined pit with a glass roof over the top, filled with a foot of fresh manure which generated heat as it rotted. Pineapples soon became essentials on top people's dinner tables, and their head gardeners were expected to come up trumps.

Where to see a working pineapple pit

The best place to see a working pineapple forcing pit today is in the walled vegetable garden in the Lost Gardens of Heligan, near St Austell in Cornwall, which has comparatively recently been restored to its Victorian glory. The pineapple pit still works on the same principle as its eighteenth-century ancestor.

OPPOSITE AND BELOW: Stowe is a magnificent example of the landscape movement. Originally designed by Charles Bridgeman, the garden features valleys, vistas, lakes, rivers and classical-style temples.

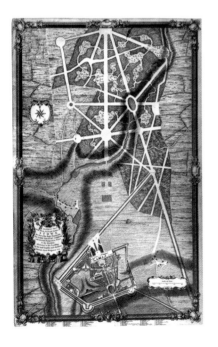

Pines (as they were known because of their pine-cone shape) were surprisingly easy to grow in pits or early greenhouses. They could tolerate a good deal of abuse as long as they didn't actually freeze in winter. Even a gardener with no previous experience could usually coax them to fruit within three years. By 1750 they were being quite widely grown, and with better greenhouses and trained staff it was possible to produce pines in half the time.

Pineapples were so fashionable that in 1761 John Murray, 4th Earl of Dunmore, had a new range of hothouses built at his Scottish home, Dunmore Park, with a smart stone penthouse on top, shaped like a giant pineapple. The whole building was heated by 'stoves' whose chimneys were disguised as Grecian urns lined up along the back wall. The roof-top fruit is now a folly, rented out as a holiday let by the Landmark Trust.

Bath and the Smart Set

The other big event in George I's reign that would indirectly affect gardens was the 'discovery' of Bath. What started the ball rolling was the visit Queen Anne had made to the town in 1702. There's nothing like royal approval for putting a place on the map. Soon the smart set began to settle in Bath for the summer season, ostensibly to 'take the waters'. (Bath contained a famous Roman spa, and great curative powers were claimed for its revolting-tasting sulphurous springs.) But the real reason for going to Bath was to see and be seen; it was the place to catch up on gossip, see all the latest fashions and do a spot of matchmaking. Much later, Jane Austen used a mixture of local gossip and her

experiences of the Bath social whirl as the inspiration for her novels; even the gardens get a mention. Jane's family moved to Bath in 1801, where they stayed for eight years. After the death of Mr Austen, the rest of the family returned to Hampshire and settled just up the road from me, at a modest cottage in Chawton, near Alton (which is now open to the public, along with its garden).

In *Pride and Prejudice* the Bennets have a wilderness in their garden; in *Sense and Sensibility* Jane comments on the current fashion for picturesque landscapes: 'I do not like crooked twisted blasted trees' she says. The picturesque style is also discussed by the Tilney family in *Northanger Abbey*, and *Mansfield Park* refers to Mr Humphry Repton, whose fees were five guineas a day (of more later).

The leader of the smart set in Bath was Richard 'Beau' Nash, who was obsessive about correct social behaviour. With a good eye for business as well as a correctly tied cravat, Beau Nash presided over the pump room, where punters could 'take the waters' in luxury, and the assembly rooms, where they could gossip, gamble, dance and flirt – all in the best possible taste.

And here's where the story veers back towards gardens. It was at Bath that the architect Robert Adam first used the warm, buff-coloured local stone to build the Royal Crescent and a particularly elegant bridge, using a brand-new architectural style that was shortly to catch on in smart gardens – Palladian.

By now all the ingredients were in place for a major change in gardening style. Aristocrats were bored with regimented, formal, foreign-style gardens. They had the awe-inspiring scenery of their grand tours for inspiration, and now they had the

architectural style to go with it. They also had the time and money to be experimental. The landscape movement was born, and the key players were already gathering in the wings.

Enter the Landscape Movement

The fashionable new 'look' for gardens was not the sort of thing that just anybody could do; you needed to be Somebody Substantial since it took a lot of land to achieve the desired effect.

'Landscaping' was much more than planting a few trees and adding a lake. It meant totally rearranging the countryside. Practitioners thought nothing of flattening entire villages and evicting the peasants, relocating rivers, reshaping hills, digging ravines and making new 'old' ruins, so that the view from a

stately home looked like a classical landscape painting with staggering 'natural' features.

Landowners used every trick in the book to make their property look more impressive. They 'stole' the view over surrounding pastures by using carefully contrived ditches, known as ha-has, instead of hedges or walls to give the impression that their land stretched as far as the eye could see. Old hunting parks were carved up into fields, and old-fashioned deer were replaced with prize-winning livestock. The writer Horace Walpole deliberately kept a dwarf breed of cows in his pastures to make his grounds look larger. And in 1763 the village of Milton Abbas in Dorset was moved a few miles to the left in order to make room for a new lake, which was needed to complete the new landscape being created for the landowner, Lord Milton, by Lancelot 'Capability' Brown.

Ha-ha – funny peculiar

ABOVE: *The ha-ha allowed landowners to 'borrow' landscape beyond their gardens by placing a drop rather than a boundary at the end of their land, such as here at The Latchett's, in Essex.*

If there's one single invention that's responsible for the success of landscape gardens, it was the ha-ha. This allowed landowners to cheat by 'borrowing' the surrounding landscape to extend their gardens.

The word 'ha-ha' is supposed to have come from the reaction of people seeing them for the first time, who'd cry 'Ah-ha!' in surprise. A ha-ha was basically a six-foot-deep ditch separating the grounds of the house from surrounding farmland. On the side nearest the garden it had a vertical face, which might be reinforced with stone or bricks to stop it collapsing. On the farmland side would be a gentle slope so that animals could graze right up to the wall without getting stuck down a steep-sided ditch or being able to jump up into the garden.

The idea of the ha-ha stems from the ancient Britons, who used defensive ditches and ramparts to fortify their hill-top encampments. French gardeners had used something similar, known as a *sal de loup* (wolf's leap), for years to keep intruders out, and one of the earliest-known ha-has in Britain was made at Levens Hall by James II's French gardener in 1690. The ha-ha became very popular as the landscape movement gained momentum.

FEATURES OF GEORGIAN GARDENS

Landscape was the defining characteristic of Georgian gardens. Depending on who you called in to lay out the grounds for you, and their particular specialities, landscape gardens might contain elements from several styles.

Gothick elements were what you might call modern-medieval. They included rustic buildings with thatched roofs, exposed timber poles, and arched window frames and doorways. This was a good style for tumbledown hermitages, brooding towers and chunks of creepy, ruined castle.

Rococo had a short, sharp spell of popularity that peaked between 1730 and 1770. It was an architectural style that was basically heavy-handed with the scrolls and curves. When translated outdoors, it produces overdecorated gardens bristling with shell-studded grottoes, and artificial caves glistening with minerals and head-banging stalactites, plus hints of chinoiserie, with elaborate borders snaking hither and thither through a slightly more formal garden structure. It's more wedding cake than rearranged landscape.

One of the best examples still around today is Painshill in Surrey. The Hon. Charles Hamilton bought the Painshill estate at the age of 34, and spent years creating an elaborate rococo garden, complete with glittering grotto and acres of ground dotted with eccentric features. He had to sell it in 1773 to pay his debts. It's still being restored.

The most outrageously over-the-top grotto still with us must be the one at Goldney Hall, a small

THE HOUSE OF HANOVER – IMPROVING ON NATURE

ABOVE: Sir William Chambers was a fan of chinoiserie and it influenced many of his designs. The most famous of these is probably the pagoda at Kew, which was completed in 1762.

OPPOSITE: Stourhead, in Warminster, was laid out in the mid-eighteenth century and exemplified the Palladian style, with elegant bridges and classical temples surrounding a central lake.

garden just outside Bristol. It's a chamber lined with shells and minerals, complete with gushing torrents and labyrinthine passages.

Chinoiserie, or mock-Chinese decoration, came into fashion between 1730 and 1740. Willow-pattern tea sets and oriental furniture were the big thing for smart drawing rooms, and all manner of Chinese junk was creeping into gardens. Sir William Chambers was a particular fan. After a business career that involved a good deal of eastern travel, he'd built up a great knowledge of oriental architecture and written a book on the subject. This inspired a career change, and he set up as an architect – his special subject, chinoiserie. The pagoda at Kew is his.

Palladian was the romantic-classical style popularized by Robert Adam in Bath, before it crept out into garden landscapes. The term 'Palladian' comes from a sixteenth-century Italian Renaissance architect, Andrea Palladio, whose works would have been seen by aristocratic young men on their grand tour. Palladio applied his own individual 'improvements' to classical Greek- and Roman-style buildings. This was the style that proved very popular for elegant bridges, ruined temples and obelisks. Classical buildings in the

Poetic licence

The poet Alexander Pope, who claimed that 'all gardening is landscape painting', had one of the first landscaped gardens at his home in Twickenham (said to be the inspiration for Prince Frederick's garden at Carlton House, of which more later). In his grounds was a fashionable grotto decorated with stalactites swiped from a real cave in Cornwall.

garden were a form of architectural ego-trip. They couldn't help displaying the landowner's good taste, culture and expensive education, but they were also meant to leave a philosophical aftertaste: romantic ruins were there to remind you of the decay that eventually overtakes all great civilizations. Dutch artists of the seventeenth century had much the same idea, and would include a butterfly or frog in their famous flower paintings to symbolize the ephemeral nature of life.

Elysian and Arcadian landscapes mean roughly the same thing – romanticized rustic scenery with ancient Greek-style outbuildings in various states of disrepair.

Elysium was the mythological paradise that the heroes of ancient Greece went to for their rewards in the afterlife. Elysian landscapes were therefore meant to be paradise on earth.

Arcadia is a mountainous area of southern Greece, which in Greek mythology is the home of Pan. Arcadian landscapes are English scenery with mythological overtones.

WHO'S WHO IN THE LANDSCAPE MOVEMENT

Charles Bridgeman (1680–1738) – ha-ha supremo
Bridgeman was the first of the great landscapers. He made his name by replacing vertical garden boundaries with sunken ha-has to let in the views, but he didn't rip out his clients' old formal gardens – he just adapted them. He'd leave the basic shape of shady walks outlined with hedges, but he'd reshape the lawns to make a more natural look, and tack on woodlands or fields so that the garden merged gradually out into the countryside. Nothing drastic.

Bridgeman originally trained as a surveyor. He worked for London & Wise for a time, and eventually became a royal garden superintendent in his own right. His star turn was laying out Stowe, in Buckingham, and also Claremont landscape garden, near Esher in Surrey, though his work was later updated, first by William Kent and then by 'Capability' Brown, so what you see there today isn't really 'his' landscape.

William Kent (1684–1748) – theatrical 'special effects'
William Kent didn't so much rearrange the landscape as redecorate it. He saw the countryside as a theatrical backdrop, with himself as set designer and nature providing the actors.

Kent had a thing about straight lines – he hated them. He turned formal canals into meandering lakes, he ripped out formal walks and made them wind romantically away into groves of trees, and his streams always snaked sinuously through valley floors.

But he is best known for his Elysian landscapes, with long vistas and mock-classical buildings used as focal points. If, today, you visit a landscape garden stuffed with ruined temples, you can bet your bottom dollar Kent designed it. Rousham Park in Oxfordshire is a gem.

Kent's background wasn't in gardening; he'd originally been an architect and artist – his early career was spent copying classical paintings for clients. (The term 'art forgery' springs to mind, but presumably it was all quite above board.) The experience came in handy as he 'saw' gardens in a different light from earthier horticulturists. Never short of special effects, he once planted some dead trees in Kensington Gardens to give his new landscape instant credibility – so perhaps there was something of the forger in him after all.

Kent was very often brought in after Bridgeman had already given the landscape a first going-over, to accentuate the new 'look'. Kent's big triumph was Stowe, the ultimate landscape garden, which at various times was worked on by virtually everyone who was anyone in landscape-garden circles. Still being restored today, its original features include a Grecian valley, Elysian fields, pheasantry, Chinese house and obelisk, all set in hundreds of acres of flowing parkland.

The diarist Horace Walpole once said of Kent: 'He leapt the fence and saw that all nature was a garden', as if he'd invented the idea, when actually Bridgeman beat him to it.

Lancelot 'Capability' Brown (1716–83) – Big Name in landscaping
'Capability' Brown gained his nickname because every time he visited a prospective client he'd comment that their grounds had 'great capabilities for improvement'.

But Brown didn't rearrange landscapes; he completely demolished them and started again. It was quite on the cards for him to move villages, as he did at Milton Abbas, and he regularly made brand-new lakes, as at Blenheim, or woods or hills. At Chatsworth he moved the village of Edensor and removed a hill which had a much better long-distance view behind it. Natural features were his stock-in-trade and he wasn't fond of fancy architecture, though he'd sometimes stretch a point and allow himself the odd rustic cow-shed.

Brown's trademark was to surround the house with a sea of grass, for contrast with parkland further away. His planting schemes always used very English-looking trees, such as elm, Scots pine, oak, larch and cedar of Lebanon. If you think his landscapes look rather stark today, it's because you aren't seeing them the way Brown planted them. Originally his groups of trees had an understorey of flowering shrubs, with banks of hollies surrounding them to act as year-round 'outlines', but they died out once the trees grew too big and created heavy shade. His landscapes were also meant to be kept neat and tidy, so the grass was cut short – not just around the house, but out in the parklands too.

By training, 'Capability' Brown was a gardener. He learnt his craft from the bottom up, starting at an estate in Scotland. He moved to

ABOVE: *Blenheim Palace is a classic example of a Capability Brown landscape.*

Stowe, where he worked for ten years before striking out on his own. Over his lifetime it's reckoned he worked on over 100 major gardens including Kew and Hampton Court. The Victorian gardening authority John Claudius Loudon said there was scarcely a country gentleman in England who hadn't consulted him at some time, and Brown once turned down a job in Ireland because, as he said, he 'hadn't finished England yet'.

Humphry Repton (1752–1818) – reintroduced 'real' gardening

Repton had failed at several businesses before turning to his hobbies (botany, natural sciences and gardening) to earn a living. Once inspiration struck, his aim was to become the natural successor to 'Capability' Brown, so he set up shop only towards the end of the great landscape-gardening boom. He often worked in partnership with the architect John Nash to offer a complete indoors-and-outdoors makeover service, and between them they worked on a good many London squares.

Repton's big contribution to garden history was to bring back the terrace so that grand country houses no longer seemed to sprout straight out of the lawns; also, landowners could once again walk round the back without getting their feet wet.

New plants were by now literally pouring into Britain from all over the world. Repton made it possible for plant-lovers to incorporate special areas for all their favourites within landscaped grounds, so you'd find rose gardens, water gardens or special areas for Chinese plants, which must have been a great relief.

Repton is famous for his 'Red Books' containing a set of watercolours with pop-up patches, which he prepared to show prospective clients 'before' and 'after' views of his proposed new landscapes. Bound in red leather, they were designed to impress. Left lying casually around, they would be seen by visitors to the house, who would be sure to admire the owner's taste, and they also acted as good advertisements for Repton's services.

Gilbert White (1720–93) – pioneer of d-i-y gardens

Not everyone had the room or the budget for a major landscape garden, but anyone with a modest space who enjoyed gardening and wanted a fashionable look – such as the clergy – would often put in their own do-it-yourself version.

The Rev. Gilbert White, who lived just up the road from me at Selborne in Hampshire, not only did so, but wrote about it in his famous epic, *The Natural History and Antiquities of Selborne* (1788). Although he's always thought of as the vicar of Selborne, he was actually the curate of a neighbouring parish – Farringdon – for most of his life. He only became curate of Selborne in 1793, when he really should have retired.

His house, The Wakes, had just an acre of 'proper' garden, plus a small orchard and a couple of fields, which he used as his 'park'. He dug his own ha-ha to open up views to the distant beech hangers and, instead of expensive statues, he made cut-out figures which, it's claimed, looked quite realistic from a distance. His kitchen garden contained a melon house covered with writing paper in place of glass, which was not only hard to come by but expensive as it was heavily taxed at the time.

A lot of Gilbert White's original garden is still there, and the rest is being re-created as it was in the eighteenth century. It is regularly open to the public.

ABOVE: *George II and his wife, Caroline, were enthusiastic gardeners.*

Stephen Duck

If you've contemplated a career as a hermit consider the CV of the most famous of the breed, Stephen Duck.

Background: From Wiltshire; earned 4/6d a week as a thresher.

Big break: 'Discovered' by one of Queen Caroline's ladies-in-waiting.

High point: Hermit to royalty; wages 11/6d per week.

Duties: Hermit-in-charge at Merlin's Cave and custodian of Duck Island, the pond in St James's Park.

Hobbies: Poet and angry young man of the agricultural scene; took much flak for suggesting that women workers sat around doing nothing.

Low point: Drowned himself in 1756.

GEORGE II, CAROLINE AND THE ROYAL GARDENS

But back to the royal soap opera. George I couldn't stand his eldest son and in 1717, after a series of big family rows, the Prince of Wales and his wife, Caroline of Ansbach, were expelled from the court. No longer welcome in the royal palaces, they moved into Leicester House in London, and two years later the Prince bought Richmond Lodge, with 100 acres of ground adjoining the river Thames, to use as their summer residence.

Caroline was keen to go garden-making as she came from a great gardening family, but she couldn't afford it until her father-in-law died and her husband inherited the throne, and with it a decent income.

When Prince George became George II in 1727, Caroline used her feminine wiles on the prime minister, her old friend Sir Robert Walpole, and charmed out of him an allowance of £100,000 a year for herself, which she spent mostly on gardens.

Her first project was to pack all her father-in-law's dangerous animals off to a zoo and get to grips with Kensington Gardens. She took in some extra land from Hyde Park, bringing the total area up to 275 acres, and brought in Charles Bridgeman to superimpose his fashionable new landscape style on the existing formal garden. A wide ditch was dug to form a deerproof boundary between Hyde Park and Kensington Gardens, to make the views seem more spacious, and Bridgeman put in winding walks and groves of trees.

William Kent joined the payroll and began working at Kensington Gardens with Bridgeman.

True to form, he introduced a few classical touches, such as obelisks and buildings, including the Queen's Temple. Then, in 1730, Bridgeman joined the ten separate ponds that had originally been made for Queen Anne years before to make one large, natural-looking stretch of water, which became known as the Serpentine – odd really, considering it's L-shaped. The soil that was dug out was disposed of ingeniously by making a 'mount', at the top of which a revolving summer-house was constructed, which could be turned to face either Kensington or St James's, depending on which particular palace you felt like looking at.

Caroline's next job was the garden at Richmond Lodge, which her husband had bought while he was Prince of Wales. She once again brought in Kent and Bridgeman to do the garden.

Here, having a virtually clean slate, they could be more creative. Starting from the house, the garden began by being fairly formal, then evolved into typical farmland fields and countryside, with pockets of woodland containing various features designed to take people by surprise. Visitors were to follow a set route round the garden so that they saw everything in the correct order.

One of the first 'surprises' was Merlin's Cave, designed by William Kent. This was no dreary hole cut into rocks; it was an elegant 'gingerbread cottage' with a trio of conical thatched roofs and Gothic windows, inside which resided a life-size waxwork of King Arthur's wizard. It even had its own real live hermit, Stephen Duck. A lot of people found the cave completely over the top, but then anything new and different often comes in for a bit of stick. At any rate, Merlin's Cave started a craze for

'hermitages' at all the more outrageous landscape gardens that were Kent's speciality.

Still following the official route around the garden, the next 'surprise' you'd encounter, tucked away in a clearing in the woods, was a ruined, classical-style temple with a bell tower. This wasn't the ruin it looked like because inside lived a collection of great men of science – or at least their busts. This was a touch of flattery meant to show off the good taste and education of the garden-owner, and again the idea was much copied at fashionable landscape gardens all round the country.

Caroline died in 1737, owing £20,000. She'd seriously overspent her gardening budget.

THE BIRTH OF KEW

Frederick, the son and heir of George II and Caroline, found himself in the same position as his father had been – heartily loathed by the King and a frequent target of family rows. So at the age of 17 he bought Carlton House in Pall Mall, with 12 acres of grounds, to use as his London residence. Shortly after this he married Augusta of Saxe-Coburg, and the pair brought in William Kent to make one of his typically theatrical gardens for them.

Although the plot was decidedly small for a landscape garden – you really needed rolling acres to do the style justice – there was room for a long

ABOVE: In its heyday Kew Palace was used as a royal residence, most notably by Frederick, heir to George II, who was responsible for landscaping the grounds around it.

vista leading out from the house through groves of
trees to a Palladian temple flanked by a pair of trellis
screens, with classical statues standing around
under umbrella-shaped specimen trees.

As heir to the throne, Frederick also needed a
country residence, so in 1729 he bought Kew House,
next to Richmond Lodge, which was owned by his
parents. Kew House had a very respectable garden, so
nothing much was done to it for 20 years, when the
Prince and Princess of Wales called in William Kent
to give the house and grounds a good going-over.
But Kent died before work could begin and, since the
other big landscape designers of the day were all off
on other jobs, it's thought that the garden was largely
planned by a good friend of Frederick and Augusta's,
Lord Bute. His lordship was a keen gardener and
amateur botanist who'd built up a serious plant
collection at Kenwood House, in Hampstead.

Kew House sat in an odd-shaped piece of land –
a long, lean triangle with a lake in the middle – so
instead of designing the garden to look out over
surrounding countryside like a typical landscape
garden of the time, the views at Kew looked inwards
towards the lake, with its small island as the focal
point. Around the lake were fields of livestock with a
bridge connecting them to the island, and the entire
garden was surrounded by a collection of rare and
exotic trees, on which the Prince and Princess of
Wales were particularly keen.

They'd planned to adorn their arboretum with
some rather eccentric decorative buildings, but only
a few of these were built in Frederick's lifetime. One
of these was the House of Confucius. This was a
one-storey building with dragon 'gargoyles'
sprouting out around a fancy roof, with bells
hanging from them. Inside, it was decorated with

tasteful scenes from the life of the oriental philosopher – the cerebral 'flattering the client' stunt that landscapers were so good at.

The Prince and Princess of Wales both took a close interest in the work going on in their grounds, but the garden was quite literally the death of Frederick. He was out one day in a rainstorm, supervising some tree-planting, when he caught a chill and died. Work stopped immediately, in 1751, with the garden unfinished, for now.

Following Frederick's death, Prince George – the eldest of Frederick and Augusta's sons – became the new Prince of Wales. At the time he was only 12 years old, and since Augusta still wasn't on friendly terms with George II, she largely brought Prince George up on her own, with her old friend Lord Bute acting as his tutor and father-figure. (Yes, there was gossip.)

George III and Kew

When George II died, in 1760, Prince George became George III. By then he'd learnt to share his mother's great love of gardens and gardening. Meanwhile, Lord Bute had quit his career in politics over the scandal of his 'association' with Augusta (he'd made it to Prime Minister for a time), and the pair of them continued developing the garden at Kew with the new King's blessing. It was in this second phase of its development that Kew really took off.

Sir William Chambers, whom Bute had once brought in to teach Augusta and the young Prince George elementary architecture, had been taken on to finish the garden, doing some designing and directing works. It seems likely that he didn't have a totally free hand – Bute and Augusta would have had plenty of suggestions of their own.

Between 1757 and 1763 Chambers put up all sorts of peculiar buildings in the grounds at Kew. Many of them were made of only wood and plaster, and some were quite literally thrown up overnight as they were never intended to last. Most eventually fell down or were demolished as unsafe, but some lasted the course. The 160-ft-tall pagoda, the orangery and the temples of Bellona and Aeolus are still there today.

Although Kew was basically a landscape garden, it was by now very fashionable for 'serious' gardens to have a botanical collection hidden away where the flowers wouldn't spoil the views. Kew was no exception. It had exotic plants, greenhouses and a pheasantry. For flowers, Sir William Chambers designed showy beds, with the tallest plants in the middle graduating down in size towards the edges,

ABOVE: *George III's big contributions to royal gardening were creating a palace out of Buckingham House, and building a cottage for his wife, Charlotte, at Kew.*

outlined with rows of the very shortest plants – which sounds to me very much like the starting point for Victorian bedding.

Augusta's botanical collection took up nine acres. William Aiton was 'poached' from the Chelsea Physic Garden to run it and give the venture more botanical 'clout' – the physic garden had a reputation for succeeding with rare plants.

In 1758 the idea of making Kew into a fully fledged Royal Botanic Garden, complete with a programme of lectures was floated. But it wasn't to happen just yet. Kew became 'royal' only when Augusta died in 1772. Her botanic garden was to go on to much greater things after her death. The recently built Princess of Wales Conservatory commemorates Augusta as founder of Kew, and not the last holder of the title, Diana, as many people assume.

GEORGE III, 'CAPABILITY' BROWN AND THE OTHER ROYAL PALACES

Meanwhile, back to George III. After he became king in 1760, at the age of 22, his mother thought it was time he had a wife and asked her friend Lord Bute to shop around for a suitable candidate. Several European princesses sounded fine on paper, but they needed looking at rather carefully. Royalty always liked to 'keep it in the family', and centuries of in-breeding had produced a number of inherited genetic problems which, not unnaturally, Augusta wished to avoid. It later turned out that George himself suffered from one – porphyria – which would eventually give rise to his well-known bouts of madness.

The lady Bute came up with was Princess Charlotte of Mecklenburg-Strelitz, who turned out to be a very good choice. Charlotte was a fair looker, a fanatical gardener, and also very keen on botany and botanical art. In 1773 a newly introduced plant was named after her – *Strelitzia reginae*, the Bird of paradise flower, from the Cape of Good Hope in South Africa.

George III inherited a buoyant country with flourishing overseas trade and an industrial revolution in full swing. The countryside was awash with cash, as farming was thriving, so landowners were reinvesting in their country estates and gardening was still going great guns. Aristocratic grand tours were now grander than ever, and Robert Adam was the fashionable architect. Conditions couldn't have been better for gardening to boom. Under George III, 'Capability' Brown was brought in to update the royal gardens. He'd already built up an impressive array of A-list clients, including Chatsworth and Blenheim, before he became Head Gardener at Hampton Court in 1764.

Hampton Court still had William III's old formal garden, allowing for the minor alterations made by

his wicked sister-in-law in the name of economy, so it might be assumed that 'Capability' Brown's first job would be to rip the lot out and replace it with one of his trademark landscapes. But he didn't. Not from any sense of history – it was quite simply because the king had been brought up there, and couldn't set foot in the place without remembering the rows that had split the family. He had no intention of living there again, so it wasn't worth spending money on the garden. For the rest of George's long reign Hampton Court was used only for grace and favour apartments for members of the royal household. And they could jolly well put up with the old garden.

However, one of 'Capability' Brown's few innovations at Hampton Court was planting the famous Great Vine, in 1769. It's a 'Black Hamburgh', now over 120 ft long and still cropping well – each year the vine keeper picks anything from 500 to 700 lb of fruit when it ripens, from early to mid-September, and baskets of grapes are sold to visitors in the Hampton Court gift shop.

Instead of redesigning Hampton Court, 'Capability' Brown was given the job of making over

the grounds of Richmond Lodge, which the royal couple also owned. Here, true to form, he obliterated Queen Caroline's old formal garden and put in a 'natural' landscape, for which he took a lot of flak from the resident gardener on the other side of the fence – Sir William Chambers, who worked at Kew House. The two of them never did get on.

When Augusta died in 1772 George and Charlotte inherited Kew House, along with its garden stuffed with Chambers's eccentric oriental buildings. With the good grounding in gardening he'd received from his mother, George oversaw the work that Sir Joseph Banks unofficially undertook at Kew. Banks's mission was to continue Augusta's work and turn her old garden into the world's top botanic garden – a mission he excelled at (see page 115). George didn't do much landscaping in the garden at Kew, however, except build a cottage for Charlotte to use as her studio-cum-retreat. The distinctive style, known as a cottage *ornée*, was 'borrowed' from France. The idea was to have a very ornate rustic shell around a luxurious interior, a style that was much copied in some landscape gardens. The Queen's Cottage is still at Kew today.

ABOVE: Queen Charlotte's cottage was used as a summer-house and still exists at the Royal Botanic Gardens, Kew, where it looks sensational in spring when the bluebells burst into flower.

Money matters

*'Capability' Brown was paid a fee of £1,107 6s for running Hampton Court.
This had to cover not only his salary, but also all the labour charges and
materials involved, so it wasn't quite so generous as it appears. He was given
an extra £100 a year specially for growing pineapples, and later St James's
Park was added to his job spec, which brought his total 'take' up to £2,000
per year – roughly half what William III had been paying.*

Buckingham House

If his mother Augusta was to be remembered as the
founder of Kew, George III's big contribution to royal
garden history was Buckingham House. He'd bought
it for the knock-down price of £28,000 in 1761, the
year after he became king. It was originally meant to
be Charlotte's dower house (the place where the
Queen did her own private entertaining, and where
she'd live if the King died first). But George decided
it would make them a good new royal palace. They
were, after all, a bit short of decent accommodation.
The burnt-out Palace of Whitehall had never been
replaced, St James's Palace and Windsor were by now
badly run-down, and George didn't want anything to

do with Hampton Court. That decided, he
commissioned Robert Adam and Sir William
Chambers to do the place up.

On the site where Buckingham Palace now
stands, there had once been a grand old mansion
called Arlington House. In 1705 a new owner
demolished the remains and built a new house on
the spot. By the time work was finished, he'd been
elevated to the title of Lord Buckingham, so he
naturally called the place Buckingham House.

Buck House was a lot smaller then than it is
nowadays, just a square 'box' looking down the Mall
with a courtyard in front. The 40-acre back garden,
designed by top society gardeners London & Wise,
had a terrace with *parterres* and fountains leading
out to rather formal grounds containing a canal
outlined with avenues of trees, and a wilderness full
of nightingales.

After the Duke of Buckingham died George II
enquired about the house, but the asking price of
£60,000 was considered far too high, and it wasn't
till 1761 that the Duke's heir finally accepted a much
lower price from George III. There was a long legal
wrangle as it transpired that part of the house had
somehow been built on land previously occupied by
James I's mulberry garden, which had belonged to
the Crown all along. Still, this probably helped to
bring the price down.

It took a year to do up the house, and the slightly
old-fashioned garden was given a minor update at
the same time. In 1763, Charlotte organized a
surprise for George in the garden – a combined
house-warming and 25th-birthday party. Robert
Adam acted as her party planner, and the garden was
filled with temporary decorations especially for the

*BELOW: Buckingham House
was built as a box-like house
in 1705. George III was the
first royal owner of the
property and put a lot of
work into alterations to the
house and garden.*

occasion, and lit up with thousands of glass lanterns. George was evidently so overwhelmed that he gave the house to Charlotte as a gift, and for a long time afterwards it was known as the Queen's House.

Buckingham House remained the couple's London residence for many years, until their increasingly large family outgrew it. In those days each member of the royal family had their own large staff to look after them, and the heir to the throne needed a complete set of apartments from quite an early age. The family eventually spent most of their time at Kew House, where new cottages were built around the green at Kew village for all the various household hangers-on. Meanwhile, to tackle the mounting housing problem, George commissioned William Chambers to design a bigger new palace for him at Richmond. Although Richmond Lodge was knocked down in readiness, the new palace was never built.

Windsor

Failing the new house at Richmond, George and Charlotte did up Windsor Castle to use as their summer residence, and as their family grew (they eventually had 15 children), they spent more time than ever there. George had much work done in the Great Park, of which he was particularly fond. His major new addition was a picturesque lake, two miles long, which was put in at the south end of the park. This had all the fashionable trimmings – a cascade, grotto, Palladian bridge, tea house and towers. Today it's better known as Virginia Water.

George also had two large farms laid out in the grounds of Windsor Great Park, with a dairy that produced all the milk and cream for the royal household. He took such a personal interest in all things agricultural that he was lampooned in the popular press as 'Farmer George', a name that stuck.

By 1788 what had begun as George's occasional 'funny turns' began to develop into long spells of more serious 'madness', so he shut himself away at Windsor. To keep the children offside during the more unpleasant episodes, Charlotte rented a cottage half a mile down the road. Originally the idea had been to do this up, but instead George bought her Frogmore – a house with some land near Virginia Water where she made herself a new garden.

Charlotte had the garden redone in typical landscape style – all meandering paths, lake, lawns and shrubberies – with a Gothic ruin and hermitage. The old vegetable patch she'd inherited with the property was turned into a spectacular flower garden, using hundreds of plants sent over specially from Kew (she was friends with the director), and a greenhouse was added later – the hallmark of a keen gardener.

Every summer Charlotte held a glamorous garden party at Frogmore, and would have the garden done up and specially decorated for each occasion. Pavilions were put up for guests to take supper in, and a temporary temple was erected on an island in the lake – which was such a hit that it was later replaced by a permanent one. To celebrate the King's Golden Jubilee in 1809 all the stops were pulled out and the garden was decorated with patriotic scenes from the Napoleonic Wars. Around 1,000 guests were fed in a real sultan's tent.

The garden at Frogmore is occasionally open, but what you will see there nowadays is Queen Victoria's version.

Outside interests

When George went through one of his 'episodes' it was considered that he was best left alone, but Charlotte had plenty to amuse her. One of her daughters, the Princess Elizabeth, shared her interest in botany and gardening. Sir Joseph Banks, the director of Kew, was a great friend, and Mrs Delaney, whose botanically accurate paper collages of the plants at Kew are part of a collection at the British Museum, was a frequent visitor. Charlotte also collected the work of Mary Moses, an artist who did a series of paintings of the flowers growing at Frogmore, which were on show in the house. It started a new craze for botanical art.

JOSEPH BANKS AND THE PLANT-HUNTERS

BELOW: Opened in 1987, the Princess of Wales Conservatory was named in honour of Augusta, Princess of Wales, and built to house a wide range of plants within its ten climatic zones; from arid to tropical.

One of the leading lights of the gardening world in the eighteenth century was the botanist Joseph Banks, who became the first director of Kew.

Born in 1743, he studied natural history and inherited a fortune at 21. After cutting his teeth on a couple of relatively minor plant-hunting trips he sailed with Captain Cook on *HMS Endeavour* in 1768, as the resident botanist on the famous round-the-world trip. Banks had in fact financed the entire voyage, which cost £10,000, and, in anticipation of some worthwhile 'finds', took with him a library of natural history books and nine assistants.

The main purpose of the trip was a three-month stopover in Tahiti so that the astronomers on board could observe the transit of Venus, but for Banks it meant plenty of time for botanizing.

From Tahiti the ship went on to New Zealand, where Banks added many new plants to his rising tally. He met *Clianthus puniceus* (glory pea) growing

in a native Maori settlement, where the locals hospitably demonstrated the correct technique for eating a human arm. On 28 April 1770 the ship dropped anchor off the eastern coast of Australia, and Banks found so many specimens that the place became known as Botany Bay.

Back home in 1772 Banks, who was the first (unofficial) director of Kew, continued Augusta's good work. His first job was to expand the plant collection, so he sent out Kew's very own plant-hunters to bring back new species from all over the world. Francis Masson returned with cinerarias and pelargonium species from South Africa; William Kerr collected plants in China; and Archibald Menzies went to North and South America. With other botanists exploring far distant countries and offering their finds when they returned, the collection built up at a cracking pace. Rare plants were highly sought after as status symbols, and landscape gardens were already being altered to make places to grow them – Humphry Repton's speciality. It was reckoned that Kew had the biggest and best botanical collection in the whole of Europe.

But Banks particularly briefed his collectors to look out for plants of economic importance. His plan for transferring tea plants from China to India, with a view to producing tea in the colonies and keeping the profits for Britain's coffers, was a winner, but it wasn't to happen for another 50 years.

All was going swimmingly until George III and Sir Joseph Banks both died in the same year – 1820. This was to prove a double whammy for Kew. Due to a lack of interest in high places, the plant collection fell into a steep decline over the next 20 years. Luckily, something happened to shoot Kew back to stardom, and we'll pick up the threads in the next chapter.

PRINCE GEORGE AND HIGH SOCIETY

Maybe it's because George III was out of action so much that his eldest son went off the rails. By the age of 16 the heir to the throne had already notched up a string of mistresses and some serious debts. Around his 21st birthday, in 1783, he moved out of the family homes and into Carlton House, where he let rip on a real playboy lifestyle – parties, gambling, women... the works.

Prince George wasn't a gardener by inclination, but gardening was fashionable and anything trendy was OK by him. The garden at Carlton House had originally been put in for his grandfather Frederick by William Kent, and clearly wouldn't do for the acknowledged leader of the smart social set. George wanted a garden that would make a grand setting for the big parties that he regularly threw, so he had it re-designed, with banks of shrubs round the sides for privacy (his parties were none too refined) and a lawn in the middle big enough to take a huge marquee.

In 1807 he had a fashionable Gothic-style conservatory built on to the house, opening out from his fashionable, Gothic-style dining room, but plants were put in there only for special occasions. Like so much else about Prince George, they were just for show. He continued to use Carlton House as his London base until it was demolished in 1827. (The Athenaeum Club is now on the site.)

The same year as he moved into Carlton House, George – who had a notoriously soft spot for 18-course dinners – went to a little fishing village called Brighton to take his stomach for a sea-water 'cure'. There he leased a house in which to keep his current mistress, a Mrs FitzHerbert, whom he had to meet

on the quiet because his parents didn't approve. Taking rather a shine to the place, he commissioned an architect to build him a better house on the same spot, overlooking the sea. It became the ultimate holiday home – Brighton Pavilion.

The architect played safe and built a fairly classical-style house but George, who was a great collector, fell in love with oriental art and kept adding new wings to display his burgeoning collection. The last straw was a huge Indian-Mogal-style stable block. Predictably, the place now looked a complete hotch-potch of styles, and was ripe for a right royal makeover.

The famous landscape gardener Humphry Repton was asked to take on the job. He needed to find a way of 'pulling together' all the various elements under one umbrella, and drew up plans for a theatrical Mughal-style fantasy, with extravagant oriental gardens to match. It would have been exactly right for the client, and Repton even produced one of his famous Red Books, but the cost of executing his plans was astronomical, so in 1814 the architect John Nash was taken on instead. His scheme featured a Mogal pavilion surrounded by a very basic garden – just lawns with groups of shrubs, some perennials and bulbs – very much the same as is there now.

George had a notoriously short attention span, and as soon as his new palace was finished he was bored and moved on to other things.

It was given a fashionable garden with all the latest trimmings – veranda, French windows with flower gardens outside, a conservatory, an aviary (exotic birds were very fashionable) and a covered walk to allow enjoyment of the garden without getting wet when it was raining. The grounds were thickly edged with dense banks of shrubs for privacy, as the Royal Lodge was by now the centre for the Prince's shocking social life. In addition, George was terrifically vain and his self-indulgent lifestyle was already catching up with him: cartoons of the time depict him as elephantine, with breeches strained to bursting point. He didn't want to give the tabloids more fuel.

OPPOSITE AND BELOW:
In 1814 John Nash was taken on as architect for the design of the Royal Pavilion, Brighton, and its garden. Nash's scheme was destroyed in the nineteenth century, but the grounds have recently been restored to their original design. Even the plant species and varieties have been selected using the original lists of plants supplied to Prince George.

GEORGE IV

In 1795 Prince George was forced to marry Caroline of Brunswick to clear his debts, but the pair were living apart within a year, and soon it was back to life as usual for the heir to the throne.

In 1811, when his father's bouts of madness finally became so severe that he couldn't continue to reign, George was appointed Prince Regent.

Prince George was unable to use Windsor Castle itself, as his father was convalescing there, but he still needed to be on hand so he found a lodge four miles away from the castle. Nash then rebuilt it for him in 1813 as a cottage *ornée* and it became the Royal Lodge.

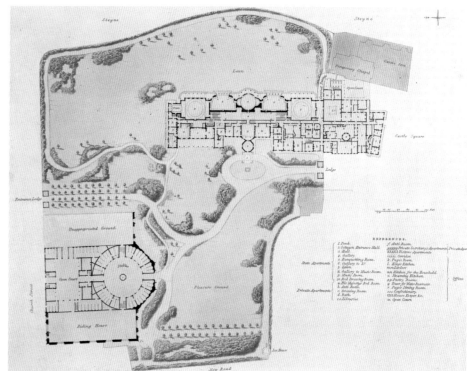

ABOVE AND OPPOSITE: In
1826 George IV set about
expanding Buckingham
House with a view to
creating a palace in which
he would live. Although
work continued under his
brother, William, it was
Queen Victoria who was
to be the first royal resident
of the newly-styled
Buckingham Palace.

After nine years as regent the prince finally
became king on his father's death in 1820. Having a
well-developed ego, he planned for himself a
typically over-the-top coronation. Among other
extravagances for his Big Day, he reinstated the
medieval tradition of having herbwomen throwing
scented foliage on the ground in front of the
monarch. But he wouldn't allow his wife Caroline
into Westminster Abbey, not even to watch the
ceremony. She was also barred from court, and so
she spent virtually the rest of her so-called marriage
living at the Ranger's House in Greenwich Park,
where one of her hobbies was growing vegetables.
Sensible woman.

George IV had Windsor Castle completely
remodelled after the death of his father. The outside
of the castle was made to look very much more

imposing, and he did up the garden, adding a
formal terrace and a sunken garden with an
orangery. Down the road at Virginia Water, where he
was fond of fishing, he had a Chinese pavilion built
on the banks at a cost of £15,000. Further along the
banks he built a ruin, using real ancient Roman
remains from the city of Leptis Magna in the Libyan
desert, which had been presented to the British
Museum. George purloined them to make his
classical feature – the museum could hardly say 'no'
to the King.

Meanwhile, back at George's old bachelor pad,
Carlton House, his collection of art and antiques
was overflowing and he urgently needed more
space. He immediately thought of Buckingham
House, and, with a view to moving his treasures in,
he hired John Nash to give it a French-style

makeover. The budget of £150,000 that Parliament allocated for the job soon soared to half a million, so Nash was promptly sacked.

The job of relandscaping the 40 acres of garden at what became Buckingham Palace was given to Repton, working in partnership with Nash as he so often did. They built three pavilions on the terrace at the back of the house, and made a picturesque landscape garden with winding walks. A fashionably natural-style lake was dug, and the soil was piled up at the end of the garden. In the centre of the garden were large, wide-open lawns so that George had room to put up his party marquees, and again he insisted on having large peep-proof banks of shrubs planted round the edge of the grounds for privacy. He was growing ever fatter, and didn't want outsiders snooping.

To make a picturesque foreground to the new-look palace, George had St James's Park freshly landscaped, and the Mall redesigned. He also put in an order for a massive and elaborate triumphal arch, with an upper storey and a statue of himself on top. Made of a rare white marble it was meant to celebrate Britain's great victories at Trafalgar and Waterloo, and he planned to put it right in front of Buckingham Palace where only the royal family would use it. But since the list of renovations to be done at the house kept growing and the costs kept adding up, the job wasn't finished and George never did move in.

Meanwhile, George's younger brother, William, Duke of Clarence, had Clarence House built as his London residence. The two men had little in common, and William didn't like throwing money around, so when George IV died and William became

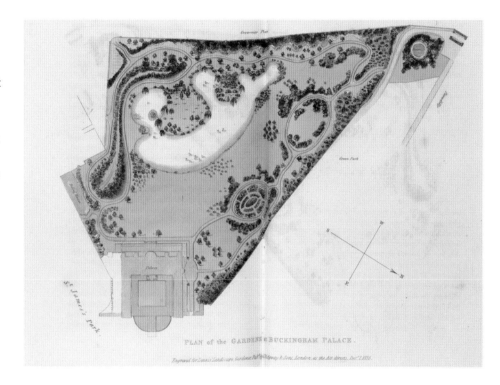

PLAN of the GARDENS of BUCKINGHAM PALACE.

the new king work on Buckingham Palace was immediately stopped. William thought the place was a great white elephant and wanted nothing to do with it. When the Houses of Parliament burnt down he offered the palace to the government, but they smelt a rat and politely declined. So William brought in a new architect, and work continued on a shoestring.

George IV's triumphal arch was an obvious economy. It was too late to cancel the order but William changed the specification to eliminate all the fancy trimming, leaving just a plain single storey. Even so, the Marble Arch still cost £100,000.

Work at Buckingham Palace was still going on when Victoria took the throne, and it eventually became her family home.

INVENTION, INTRODUCTIONS AND INGENUITY

A RECORD REIGN

Victoria, born 1819

Married Albert of Saxe-
   Coburg-Gotha 1840

Celebrated golden jubilee 1887

Died 1901

OPPOSITE TOP: The Victorian Age was a time of great technological advancement and increased wealth for some, which had a beneficial effect on gardening through tools, plants and design.

OPPOSITE BELOW: Queen Victoria had spent happy summer holidays on the Isle of Wight as a child and when choosing a new royal residence she opted for Osborne House.

Queen Victoria's reign was the longest in British history – 64 years – during which time Britain was the world power, with thriving overseas colonies that generated the money to build railways, roads and suburbs, and generally raise living standards. The Industrial Revolution was in full swing, business was expanding rapidly and bringing wealth – and jobs – to the towns, but the countryside was going downhill fast. Between 1800 and 1830 the population had doubled, and when Victoria became queen it stood at 16 million. For the rapidly expanding middle classes there were great opportunities for keeping up with – or ideally overtaking – 'the Joneses'.

Instead of making the usual royal marriage of convenience, Victoria found romance. She proposed to her cousin Albert after falling in love at first sight during a ball at Windsor Castle. But it wasn't just fate. Their respective relatives had put in a good deal of spadework behind the scenes to engineer the situation, in the hope that it would bear fruit. As it turns out, this unusual turn of events was to have a surprising impact on royal gardening history.

Victoria and Albert were a great double act. They had a lot in common and shared all their main interests. Victoria had a strong sense of family, and her reign was a time of rigid etiquette and high moral standards. While she dealt with her official paperwork, Albert – who never really had a 'proper' job – provided behind-the-scenes back-up and interested himself in good works. He was a great fan of science and technology, and was the driving force behind the Great Exhibition of 1851. On the domestic front, he took personal charge of the royal home-improvement projects – particularly the gardens.

There had never been a more exciting time to be gardening. New scientific achievements led the way to new opportunities. Glasshouses and conservatories were soon all the rage, paving the way for exotic orchids and 'hothouse' or 'stove' plants, and displays of all the new pot plants such as fuchsias and calceolarias. Bedding plants took off, bringing spectacular new planting schemes and gaudy colours that had never been seen before. There was nothing natural about Victorian gardening – it was all about putting nature firmly in its place.

VICTORIAN RESTORATION

When Victoria came to the throne the royal palaces and their gardens were in a dreadful mess. George IV's chronic overspending had left a black hole in the coffers, which William IV had tried to plug the easy way – by axing everything he could. As a result, things were by now neglected and badly run.

In the first year of Victoria's reign an urgent inquiry was held. The outcome was that central government took over all the royal palaces and their gardens. Hampton Court, Kew, St James's Palace, Kensington Palace, Windsor Castle and Buckingham Palace would all be maintained from public money, with civil servants making the decisions, though the royal family could still use parts of Buckingham Palace and Windsor, including Frogmore, and Victoria had inherited Brighton Pavilion.

Not surprisingly, Victoria and Albert decided to buy two new family homes of their own – Balmoral Castle in Scotland and Osborne House on the Isle of Wight.

Victoria had always been very fond of the Isle of Wight, as she'd often been there for summer holidays as a child, so when a Georgian property, Osborne House, with attractive grounds and sea views, came up for sale in 1844 she and Albert bought it, along with a couple of neighbouring farms to bump up the acreage.

Albert took charge of doing up the house and garden. His grand tour had left an impression, and he decided to rebuild the house as a rather solid, chunky version of the grand classic-style villas he'd seen in Italy, with a garden to match. It started a new craze. Rashes of small, Osborne-inspired Victorian villas sprang up in cities and suburbs all round the country.

On one side of Osborne House Albert had large raised terraces built, where Victoria liked having breakfast in summer – the 'day job' kept her indoors so much and she liked her fresh air. From the terraces, steps led down into a formal, Italian-style garden decorated with fountains, urns and fashionable new geometric flowerbeds, which were filled with thousands of bedding plants – usually geraniums and heliotrope.

Round the other side of the building an avenue of trees was lined up with the centre of the house, heading out into the parkland that Albert had planted. To make sure his main trees were properly placed, it's said that he used to climb up on to the roof for a bird's-eye view before issuing his instructions by waving flags.

Victoria was very keen on flowers but, as she and the family were in residence only for the summer holidays and a few special social occasions, they

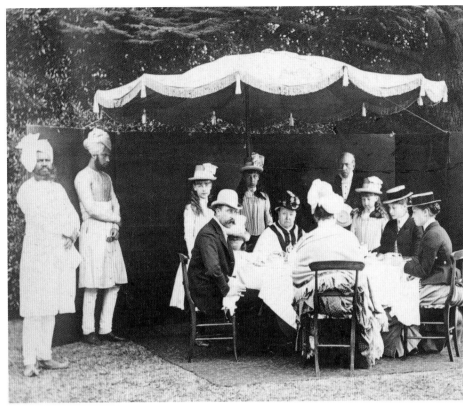

OPPOSITE: Influenced by his grand tour, Prince Albert designed an Italian garden at Osborne House, complete with classical terraces and fountains.

ABOVE: Queen Victoria loved fresh air, and what better way to enjoy it than with a garden party at one of her favourite residences, Osborne.

concentrated on plants that would be at their best when they'd be there to enjoy them. The Queen kept a diary all her life, and often noted what was out in the garden. Scented flowers, such as *Magnolia grandiflora*, jasmine, roses and honeysuckle, were among her favourites, and she also liked having lots of cut flowers indoors. But it seems that the garden at Osborne looked rather dismal in winter on the rare occasions when the family was there out of season.

The great innovation at Osborne was the children's garden. In 1853 Albert had a chalet built in the grounds, something like a grown-up Wendy house, where the children were given lessons in cookery and gardening. Each child had an identical gardening outfit, pint-sized garden tools and an equal-sized plot of ground – even royal children

have to be treated exactly the same or you never hear the last of it. They grew fruit and vegetables, and were expected to look after their gardens properly. For some of them it was the start of a lifelong love of gardening. The children's garden is still at Osborne House today, and it's a great attraction for tourists.

Victoria and Albert were very smitten with Scotland after making a couple of official visits, so when they heard that Balmoral Castle in Aberdeenshire was available they bought it.

Albert was fond of Balmoral because it reminded him so much of his old home back in Germany – all remote, rugged scenery and dark, earthy forests – while Victoria loved its romantic fairy-tale atmosphere. And it was far enough from London to really get away from it all.

LAWNMOWERS

ABOVE: Shanks's pony-pulled mower was used on the lawns at grand estates, including Queen Victoria's gardens at Balmoral.

Amazing though it sounds, until 1830 lawns were cut with a scythe. But that changed after Edwin Beard Budding invented the lawnmower. He worked in the textile industry, and borrowed the idea from a machine that 'shaved' fabric, giving it a smooth pile.

The result was advertised in gardening magazines as 'amusing, useful and healthy exercise', accompanied by an artist's impression of a dapper gent in frock coat and top hat pushing a rather Heath Robinson sort of machine. With a fairly narrow cutting width, it was only of use for small town or suburban gardens, so it was perfect for the new middle classes and by 1858 some 7,000 machines had been sold.

For grander establishments a bigger model was clearly called for, and in 1841 Alexander Shanks of Arbroath registered his pony-pulled mower that not only cut the grass, but also cleared up the clippings – and presumably anything that the pony left behind. To avoid leaving hoofprints over the lawn, the pony wore soft leather boots.

Conventional gardening was almost impossible at Balmoral, so Albert wisely decided that instead of fighting the conditions he'd let the natural landscape dictate the style – always a good idea when you're trying to garden on a 'problem site'. His method of designing was typically practical. He drew a plan of the estate in sand with his finger, and used it to 'test out' several different ideas.

INVENTION, INTRODUCTIONS AND INGENUITY

LEFT: *Balmoral, in Aberdeenshire, was another royal residence acquired by Queen Victoria. She loved its romantic feel and Albert loved its dark, rugged scenery. In keeping with the less than ideal gardening conditions, Albert allowed this garden to find its own, natural style. The herbaceous borders are a later addition at the instigation of the Duke of Edinburgh.*

Since the grounds already had conifer plantations with walks running through them, Albert accentuated what was already there to make an ornamental forest effect, which Victoria decorated with stone memorials commemorating various family events. Close to the castle walls Albert put in some lawns, and instead of risking flowers, which would quickly have been bashed to bits by the wind or eaten by deer, he made beds from tough evergreens, with sculptures of the local woodland wildlife. Although it wasn't what you'd call a conventional garden, it was exactly right for the place and eminently practical.

The big innovation Victoria introduced to Balmoral was one of the very first lawnmowers – a Shanks's pony-powered model.

RIGHT: *Glasshouses were becoming more affordable for the middle classes. They provided much-needed protection for the new exotic species finding their way into Britain.*

Guano

Guano was seagull droppings, collected from well-matured, 100-ft deep deposits that had built up on islands around the coast of Peru and Chile. It was first used as fertilizer by the Incas in the thirteenth century. From 1840 it was imported on a huge scale into Britain, and remained in use until stocks ran out. A rich source of nitrogen and phosphates, guano was powerful stuff which gardeners regarded as 30 times stronger than horse manure.

ADVANCES IN HORTICULTURE

There were many other developments in horticulture, as the rapidly growing Victorian middle classes wanted cheap copies of consumer goods that until now had been available only in expensive handmade form. This presented a golden opportunity for the new mass-production methods being developed, for greenhouses, garden products, decorations and sundries as well as plants.

Greenhouses

Large, heated glasshouses, or greenhouses, at last became a practical possibility, thanks to the invention of cast iron for making long, strong girders. (John Claudius Loudon invented the curvilinear cast-iron sash bar in 1818.) Steam boilers and cast-iron hot-water pipes for heating were soon available, and small, handmade pieces of glass gave way to large sheets when a new process was invented. The tax on glass was removed in 1845, causing the price to fall by over three-quarters to 2d per foot. As a result, Queen Victoria ordered glasshouses for her gardens at Osborne House, large nurseries sprung up outside big cities to provide bedding plants in bulk, and at last greenhouses and conservatories fell within the grasp of the middle classes.

Garden Products and Sundries

Potteries were by now able to mass-produce clay flowerpots and decorative containers for indoor gardening; a basket-weave pattern was very popular. Urns and statues were also being mass-made and sold through catalogues – even Prince Albert sent off for some garden ornaments for the grounds at Osborne House.

Cast iron was used for making garden seats and tables and decorations were made from wrought iron. A far bigger range of garden tools was available, including specialist items, such as 'wheeled engines' for spraying fruit trees. Rubber hosepipes had been invented, and wire netting first appeared around 1850.

A huge range of garden products was now in use. For fertilizers there were guano, blood, bone, horns, leather leftovers, feathers, skin, blubber and 'night soil' (all organic, if repulsive), as well as old faithfuls such as seaweed, soot and animal manures. For 'chemical' fertilizers there were various forms of lime, soda and iron sulphate. The newly invented superphosphate was made by treating bones with sulphuric acid, which doubled their fertilizer value.

Pesticides and weedkillers were quite basic. Gishurst compound, a mixture of flowers of sulphur and soap, was used as a winter wash, while mildew was treated with a mixture of lime water and urine, which was superseded by Bordeaux mixture only in 1885. Some products were lethal, such as the nicotine used against aphids and similar pests, and arsenic which was used as a weedkiller.

Plants

No longer content with what nature provided Victorian hybridizers improved on wild species, creating enormous numbers of new named varieties in the gaudy colours made fashionable by the new synthetic dyes that were taking the textile industry by storm.

The first orchid was hybridized in 1856, and cinerarias and calceolarias were 'in'. Fuchsias shot into fashion after a Mr Story bred the first hybrid with red-and-white flowers, which he named 'Victoria' in honour of the Queen.

New varieties would often sell for as much as a guinea each, a fortune at the time. Standard fuchsias were specially sought after for conservatory decoration as they didn't take up too much room. Pelargoniums were great favourites with many varieties, such as 'Paul Crampel', 'Mrs Henry Cox' and 'Crystal Palace Gem', arriving on the scene.

These and many other Victorian favourites are still available from specialist nurseries today.

Rose-breeding was at its peak, with many new varieties of what we call 'old-fashioned roses' coming from France, including favourites such as the blowsy, highly-perfumed 'Mme Isaac Pereire', and the tea-scented, buff-orange 'Gloire de Dijon'. The pink Bourbon rose 'La Reine Victoria' (after the Queen), came out in 1872. Hybrid perpetuals appeared, famous for flowering over most of the summer instead of a short sharp burst, and by 1867 the French breeder Guillot was crossing them with tea roses to produce the first hybrid teas. Between 1850 and 1870 the number of varieties increased five times over.

LEFT: *New technology brought in smaller-scale inventions for gardeners on large estates, including more convenient methods of applying pesticides – such as Mr Vermorel's Knapsack Pump.*

ABOVE AND RIGHT: Not to be outdone by her subjects, Queen Victoria ordered glasshouses for her garden at Osborne House.

*John Claudius Loudon
was the Victorian
gardening authority, and
did a great deal to
popularize gardening for
the masses. He founded*
The Gardener's
Magazine, *and wrote
many books. The*
Suburban Gardener
and Villa Companion
*(1838) was one of the
first books to cater
specially for the rising
tribe of town gardeners.*

*His wife, Jane, did
her bit to encourage
ladies to go in for indoor
gardening and, as a
result, it became quite a
fad. All sorts of over-the-
top indoor conservatories
were built, complete
with plants, aquariums
and songbirds. The
Victorians never did
things by halves.*

POLLUTION-PROOF PLANTING

London had become increasingly polluted over the centuries, but by Victorian times the coal fires used for heating and cooking were causing long-lasting smogs. Soot turned buildings black and covered gardens; eyewitness accounts describe it falling in flakes like black snow. Children developed rickets because they lacked vitamin D, normally provided by sunshine.

Right from the turn of the century, the gardening authority John Loudon had been recommending plane trees for planting in London squares, since they not only shed their leaves annually, but a lot of their bark also peels off, which gets rid of the soot. Soon, over half the trees in London were planes.

Other smoke-and-smog-resistant plants recommended for London gardens were *Rhododendron ponticum, Aucuba japonica* (spotted laurel) and privet for hedges. In fact, all three went on to become Victorian town-garden favourites.

Although the sulphur fumes from burning coal were a good cure for black spot (the fungus delights in pure air), roses had a problem surviving London pollution and were sometimes grown under bell jars for protection. Many years later, when big cities became smokeless zones and trains ran on electricity instead of coal, gardeners were tremendously indignant to find black spot once again afflicting their roses. The latest 'green' remedy? Sulphur! (But this time, out of a bottle.)

ABOVE: *Rhododendrons were perfect for Victorian town-gardens, both to provide colour and for their pollution-proof properties.*

In the south of France, nurseryman Monsieur Latour-Marliac was having great success breeding the notoriously difficult waterlilies. A lot of his varieties are still grown today, though they were produced with country-house lakes in mind and can overpower today's pocket-hanky ponds.

Fruit and vegetables weren't to be left out. Several apple varieties that are still firm favourites today were either bred or discovered in Victorian gardens. 'Bramley's Seedling' grew from a pip in a Nottinghamshire cottage garden, where it was talent-spotted by a nurseryman and named after the then owner; 'Cox's Orange Pippin' was bred by a retired brewer, Richard Cox, living near Slough; and 'Worcester Pearmain', 'Beauty of Bath' and 'Lane's Prince Albert' all appeared in Victoria's reign. The 'Victoria' plum was discovered in a Sussex garden and marketed by a Brixton nurseryman in 1844; 'The Czar', bred by the famous Rivers nursery, was named to commemorate the visit of the Tsar of Russia, a close relative of Victoria and Albert.

Some of the seed firms, such as Sutton's, were already in business supplying flower and vegetable seeds. William Thompson of Ipswich (later to unite with Mr Morgan) issued his first seed catalogue in 1855; Unwin's started up after the end of Victoria's reign, in 1903, specializing in sweet peas. A few Victorian varieties can still be found in today's seed catalogues thanks to a recent revival in 'heritage' flowers and vegetables. They include 'Green Windsor' broad bean, 'Painted Lady' runner bean with red and white bicoloured flowers, 'Purple Cape' broccoli, and, among the bedding plants, French marigold 'Tall Scotch Prize', asters 'Ostrich Feather' and 'Truffaunts Peony', and double-flowered 'Duplex' sweet williams.

*Where to see
Victorian bedding*

*One of the best places to
see Victorian bedding in
full flow nowadays is
Waddesdon Manor,
Buckinghamshire, built
by Baron Ferdinand de
Rothschild. Each
summer it takes
100,000 plants to fill
the Victorian parterres,
planted to a design now
generated by a
computer instead of the
original geometry-
trained garden staff.*

THE VICTORIAN BEDDING BONANZA

Around the 1830s enormous numbers of tender
summer-flowering plants were arriving from
Mexico, South America and South Africa, which the
Victorians planted out temporarily in beds for
summer colour and then threw away.

Bedding, as it was called, was very practical for city
gardens, especially in London where the great
concentration of coal fires meant that plants were
soon caked in soot. Only the toughest evergreens
survived for long, but the great advantage of bedding
plants was that they were regularly replaced.

London parks were soon using two million
bedding plants every year for their elaborate
showpiece schemes. Bedding was also popular with
owners of summer homes, as it meant that the
gardens looked their best for the family holiday and
could be forgotten for the rest of the year.

Very showy, formal planting schemes became
fashionable, and the Victorians had several versions.
One was rather like a floral knot garden. A round or
rectangular bed was outlined with several rows of
short bedding plants, and filled in with larger kinds,
such as pelargonium, heliotrope, lobelia, calceolaria
and salvia. Tall flowers, such as canna, were then
used as 'dot' plants in the middle to add height.
This style was very much in vogue early on in
Victoria's reign.

More striking geometric shapes came in later.
Circles (the favourite shape) were divided up into
arcs and segments, each planted with a different
kind of flower and, for extra complexity, the outlines
could be picked out with – often – a single kind of
foliage plant. Gardeners had to learn geometry in

order to lay out the shapes and mark them out
accurately; there was nothing worse than a
geometric bed that was slightly 'out'.

Another development was specialist borders in
varying shapes and sizes. One type of flowerbed was
created to look like a bouquet of flowers inside a
basket, with iron hoops woven together to form the
'wicker' sides, and soil mounded up in the middle
and planted with concentric rings of flowers. Ribbon

LEFT: Waddesdon Manor in Buckinghamshire is an impressive garden and one in which you can view the Victorian bedding-style at its most bold and showy.

borders were narrow, with regimented rows of plants lined up parallel to the sides to form stripes in contrasting colours.

Carpet bedding came in slightly later, peaking in the 1870s and 1880s. This used low-growing coloured foliage plants to make elaborate patterns, which in grand houses might include the family crest. Plants for this job had to be either naturally compact – succulents such as echeverias were ideal – or they had

to stand regular clipping to keep them short and neat; alternanthera was the great favourite.

But new ideas were needed all the time. Floral clocks were a passing fad, using flowers that opened and shut at different times of day. To get the timings right, gardeners would look up plants in a textbook. John Claudius Loudon made a list of them, along with their opening and closing times, in his *Philosophica Botanica* if you fancy having a go yourself.

ABOVE: *Under Victoria and Albert the Marble Arch was moved from its position outside Buckingham Palace to improve the view. It was positioned surveying Hyde Park where it remains today.*

finished just in time for Victoria and Albert to use their new photo-opportunity balcony to wave down to the crowds after the opening of the Great Exhibition in Hyde Park.

IMPROVING THE ROYAL PALACES

Balmoral and Osborne House were fine for holidays but for the serious job of ruling the country, Victoria needed a London base, so right from the start of her reign she moved into Buckingham Palace.

As their family increased they needed more space. The prime minister, Sir Robert Peel, felt he couldn't make money available for alterations, so Victoria sold off Brighton Pavilion (which she'd never much liked) and sank the money into Buckingham Palace. Extra nurseries, guest rooms and a big ballroom were built, and a lot of George IV's oriental treasures from Brighton Pavilion ended up decorating the newly enlarged Buckingham Palace.

Albert involved himself with some of the improvements. His interest in new technology lay behind the installation of flush loos in place of the previous primitive arrangements. And it was his idea to add the now-famous balcony to the front of the house, from which the royal family are always filmed waving.

But to make the most of the views, Marble Arch had to be moved. You'll remember that it had been plonked down right outside the palace, as per George IV's instructions. The arch was duly dismantled, and each stone was individually numbered and stacked in St James's Park, until it could be re-erected at Hyde Park Corner, where it still stands. The work was

THE GREAT EXHIBITION

The Great Exhibition of 1851 was Albert's greatest achievement. Designed to show off the latest Victorian technology and generally boost the British Empire, it took place in a purpose-built exhibition centre – a giant 'conservatory' known as the Crystal Palace – which was built in Hyde Park close to where the Albert Hall now stands. The revolutionary building was designed by Joseph Paxton, who'd already built the great conservatory at Chatsworth for his boss, the Duke of Devonshire.

The Crystal Palace must just about have qualified as the eighth wonder of the world. It was three times the size of St Paul's Cathedral, used nearly a million square feet of glass, and 2,260 men took seven months to put it up.

The exhibition was open from May to October in 1851, and was a huge success. Nearly a third of the population – over six million people – visited it, each paying 1 shilling a head. The sooty London air soon took its toll on the state of the glass. As cleaning was a king-sized headache, the Crystal Palace was dismantled in 1853 and moved out to Sydenham, where the air was cleaner, and was rebuilt half as big again. Although the area is still called Crystal Palace, the building eventually became impossibly expensive to maintain, and was finally destroyed by fire in 1936. Only stone balustrading and a bust of Sir Joseph Paxton give away any trace of its presence.

OPPOSITE: *The now destroyed Crystal Palace hosted the Great Exhibition of 1851 which displayed the latest scientific and technological advances inside a showpiece of Victorian engineering.*

The Buckingham Palace garden

Plans were afoot to construct a big new Italianate garden behind Buckingham Palace, but Victoria rejected the idea. Settling for a few minor modifications, the soil mound left behind when George IV's lake was dug was made into a feature by parking a summer-house on top. (It was pulled down in 1928.) The lake caused a minor panic in 1841 when it froze over. As Albert skated on it he fell through the ice, but fortunately escaped with just a chill.

Windsor Castle and Frogmore

Victoria had always liked Windsor. On a visit as a child she'd met the black sheep of the family, George IV, and, to her mother's horror, the young princess thought he was great fun. It was also at Windsor that she fell in love with Albert; the couple honeymooned in the castle, and spent a lot of time there later.

Albert took a particular interest in the grounds at Windsor, and became Ranger of the Great Park. He had new cottages built, with all mod cons, for the workers on the royal estate, and each year Victoria and Albert held a big Christmas party for them and their families at the castle. It was at one of these that Albert first introduced Christmas trees to Britain.

Since pagan times, our ancestors had always brought evergreens indoors to celebrate the winter solstice. Their leafy branches were supposed to house the spirits of the forests, who were invited to share the festivities for good luck. That's why we still have a fairy at the top of the Christmas tree today.

When Christianity arrived the Church banished pagan symbols like mistletoe (which had strong associations with the Druids) and the winter solstice celebration was replaced with a new religious festival – Christmas.

We still used evergreens like holly, ivy and even the dreaded mistletoe, but the idea of a decorated fir tree to put presents under was an old German custom.

The original Victorian Christmas tree decorations were fairly simple, they consisted of real candles, ribbons, nuts, fruit, sugarplums and small presents. The first glass baubles were imitation fruit and pine cones, hand-made in Prince Albert's home state of Saxe-Coburg-Gotha. By the very end of Victoria's reign they were being mass-produced, imported and sold in bulk by the founder of the well-known chain store, F.W. Woolworth.

As part of the rationalization of the royal garden, a giant kitchen garden complex was built behind Queen Charlotte's house at Frogmore. Thanks to the new steam railways, it was now considered easier to send fresh produce to wherever the royals were staying than to run a separate kitchen garden at each residence. One big kitchen garden, it was hoped, would mean big savings in costs.

The royal 'greengrocery department' at Frogmore covered 30 acres. The 12-ft-high walls surrounding it were used for growing trained fruit trees. Inside there were huge areas of salads and vegetables for all seasons, and a massive block of south-facing hothouses almost a thousand feet long produced out-of-season fruit, exotic vegetables and mushrooms. Orchid houses and ferneries provided the wherewithal for buttonholes and table decorations, and palm houses supplied fashionable potted plants. Live-in accommodation was provided for the gardeners in rows of almshouse-like cottages, and right in the middle stood the head gardener's house from which he could keep an eye on his staff of 150. Those were the days.

Joseph Paxton

Joseph Paxton first worked at the Horticultural Society's gardens at Chiswick, and was soon on nodding terms with one of the regular visitors, the Duke of Devonshire and first president of the society, who lived next door at Chiswick House. The duke's other house was Chatsworth and, finding himself short of a head gardener in 1826, just as he was due to go off on a trip, he offered the job to Paxton.

Ever keen, the young Paxton arrived at 4.30 in the morning and had to climb over the garden wall to get in. The grounds at Chatsworth were somewhat run-down, but things soon perked up. Paxton constructed a huge rockery that took two years to build and involved shifting pieces of rock weighing over 300 tons – rockeries were a great Victorian passion. But Paxton's great contribution to the landscape was the one-acre conservatory that he designed with help from Decimus Burton (who later designed the Palm House at Kew). Building started in 1836 and it took 500 men four years to complete the work. In order to keep the Great Conservatory warm enough for the collection of tropical exotics it housed it had eight boilers, fed by coal from an underground tramway so that all the workings were kept out of sight. It was quite something. When Queen Victoria visited in 1843 she drove right through the conservatory in her horse-drawn carriage.

Paxton pulled strings to obtain rare tropical plants to stock the conservatory, but none was rarer or weirder than the one that was given to him by William Hooker, the new director of Kew. It was a giant water lily from the Amazon region that grows a ring of massive round leaves, each 6ft across. Each leaf floats on a series of large geometrically arranged ribs armed with spikes underneath to deter vegetarian fish, leaving a completely flat surface above the water. The leaves are so buoyant that a full-grown one is able to bear the weight of a small child.

Paxton's plant flowered at 2 p.m. on 2 November 1849 – the first time it had been seen in Britain – beating the plants at Kew, which was a great feather in his cap. He presented a leaf and flower to Queen Victoria and the plant was named *Victoria regia* in her honour. It has since been renamed *Victoria amazonica*. You can still see specimens growing in the Princess of Wales Conservatory at Kew today. The floating flowers are white, measuring up to three feet across, and last for only two days before turning pink and sinking below the water.

The big problem Paxton found with growing his giant Amazon water lily was that the plant needed a very wide stretch of water to open out fully, and Victorian glasshouses needed a lot of internal support posts to hold the roof up. So he set about designing a new glasshouse especially for it. The structure of the water-lily leaves themselves provided the inspiration for his novel single-span structure. He later used the same idea on a much larger scale to design the Crystal Palace, for which he was knighted by Queen Victoria.

Although he had a good many better job offers – including one to become head gardener at Windsor – Paxton continued working at Chatsworth until the Duke's death in 1858. The Great Conservatory lasted until 1920, when the cost of upkeep became too great and it was pulled down. Paxton eventually became a millionaire through his commercial interests, which included small greenhouses for amateurs.

BELOW: The gardeners at Chatsworth, in front of Joseph Paxton's lily house.

A Victorian plantsman's garden

Biddulph Grange, Stoke-on-Trent, Staffordshire, was planted in high Victorian style by James Bateman, a passionate collector who created areas for different plants that needed special conditions. The garden contains Chinese gardens with their own 'Great Wall of China', a Chinese bridge as on willow-pattern plates, a joss house and a dragon parterre; a Little Egypt (right) complete with pyramid; and a grotto with stumpery, a bog garden and a fern collection. It's recently been restored to its full glory by the National Trust.

VICTORIAN OBSESSIONS

Although bedding plants were the Big New Thing in Victorian gardens, and very popular with the middle classes, that doesn't mean to say all the large landowners with last century's landscape gardens on their hands suddenly ripped the lot out and turned vast acreages over to carpet bedding. That would have been far too impractical, not to say expensive. By way of modernizing they'd put a few impressive parterres around the house, but elsewhere the trend started by Humphry Repton continued, and more specialist areas for particular plants were added to existing parkland gardens. Thanks to the masses of new plants becoming available, Victorian plant-fanciers with space to 'play' with were now able to dabble with all sorts of fantastic features.

Rockeries

The Victorian era was the heyday of the rockery, and 1860–70 was the absolute peak of the craze. By now the glittering geological grottoes of the eighteenth century had given way to much more natural-looking features that presented a golden opportunity for more eccentric aristocrats to go overboard on attention to detail.

At Hoole House near Chester, Lady Broughton ordered a mountainous rockery that was like a relief map of the Chamonix Valley in the Alps, complete with quartz glacier. Sir Charles Isham's 'rock cliff' at Lamport Hall, Northamptonshire, was perforated with caves in which china gnomes mined for crystals stuck in the walls, all landscaped with dwarf conifers so as to be in scale with their surroundings.

Ice houses

A lot of town houses by now had gas for lighting, but facilities were still fairly primitive in grand country houses, which were too far from the beaten track to be connected to mod cons. To keep food fresh ice boxes were used in the kitchens, and in order to keep the boxes supplied with the vital ingredient there'd be an ice house down the garden.

The ice house was rather like a man-made cave, sunk into the ground with a thick layer of soil over the top for insulation. There was often a 'trapdoor' in the top, through which incoming ice was shovelled, a drain in the bottom. Staff came and went with buckets to restock the kitchen ice box.

The ice house was supervised by the head gardener. In winter it would be cleaned out, and when the lake froze over the outdoor staff would be sent to cut blocks of ice, which were smashed up and stored inside. For convenience, the ice house would usually be sited fairly close to the lake, surrounded by shady trees to help keep the contents cool. The ice house of at least one stately home was reputedly still in use as late as 1930.

ABOVE: In the days before fridges, ice houses were the Victorian solution to keeping food fresh. They were built in the grounds of larger properties, but were often concealed so as not to be an eyesore.

Tourists evidently turned up by the charabanc-load. Sir Frank Crisp's rockery at Friar Park, Henley-on-Thames, beat the lot. It occupied three acres, used 7,000 tons of rock and contained a scale model of the Matterhorn with alabaster snow on top, a grotto made of Pulhamite (a kind of artificial stone made of Portland cement beefed up with crushed bricks, clinker and similar rubble – it's much the same principal as today's reconstituted paving and walling stone, which is made from rock or stone that's been ground up and 'stuck back together') and lakes illuminated with electric lights, and was colonized by herds of china mountain goats. The place was later owned by one of the Beatles.

But not all Victorian rockeries were so offbeat. The one at Kew, which was started around the same time, was far more tasteful, being made of huge limestone rocks carefully arranged so as to re-create natural strata.

What was fine on a large scale, I'm sorry to say, didn't quite work when it was copied in miniature with a tight budget, in suburban gardens. The middle classes would just heap up soil and bung in broken china, old bricks and lumps of clinker from the kitchen boiler. The gardening writer, Shirley Hibberd was heard to remark that he wished rockeries had never been invented. A rising rock-gardening star, Reginald Farrer, was very scathing about 'almond puddings', 'plum buns', 'dogs' graves' and 'sham stalactites' and wasn't at all keen on 'acres of Portland cement' – he was having a 'dig' at Pulhamite. A bank clerk, rock-plant addict, plant hunter and amateur nurseryman from Yorkshire, Farrer's rules for making a natural-looking rockery were very simple. Take a few very large chunks of rock, and turn them round so the widest side faces down, then bury them deeply like icebergs – 90 per cent out of sight. Add natural features like screes and moraines, as you find alongside real-life mountains, and a few rare plants, and Bob's your uncle. His *The English Rock Garden* is still a gardening classic today.

Fruit

Thomas Rivers of Sawbridgeworth, Hertfordshire, was mightily impressed with the trained fruit trees he saw on a visit to France, so he worked out ways of growing dwarf trees in pots so that they could be 'forced' into fruiting out of season in orchard houses, which he also invented. The idea was taken up in many of the walled gardens at grand country houses. Besides the obvious benefits, there was a good deal of kudos to be had from your head gardener being able to outshine the head gardeners of your friends. A Thomas Rivers-style orchard house has recently been reconstructed in the kitchen garden at Audley End House, near Saffron Walden in Essex. The Rivers Nursery, which specialized in fruit, continued until well into the twentieth century. Some of its stock was taken over by Reads Nursery at Loddon in Norfolk, which now supplies a huge number of rare old Victorian glasshouse fig and grape varieties, as well as other interesting 'antique' fruit.

Indoor Plants and Cut Flowers

The Victorians liked to make big indoor displays by banking up exotic potted plants on tables with moss, and this job would be done by the gardeners at big houses, particularly for special occasions, such as big dinner parties and family Christmases. For frightfully grand receptions it wasn't unknown to have the conservatory transformed into a 'rockery', using huge chunks of ice banked up and decorated with potted ferns.

In suburban living rooms Wardian cases were popular for growing ferns and other shade- and humidity-loving species, since few plants other than typically indestructible Victorian aspidistras would survive the dry air and gas fumes of a town living-room. Well-brought-up Victorian young ladies would press wild flowers, or arrange dried flowers under

glass domes as decorations and, rather morbidly, they'd make flower pictures out of tufts of hair from dear departed relatives.

The language of flowers was used in bouquets to send 'coded messages' to and from secret admirers, but both parties needed a 'code book' explaining the true meaning of every flower as it was easy to get the wrong end of the stick. Cut flowers, however, were hardly used, though Mrs Loudon broke the mould by arranging cut flowers instead of the usual stove plants in her living rooms.

Roses

The rosarium, or rose garden, came back into fashion and roses were grown as bushes, and trained as standard 'trees' up posts and pillars and out along chains, festoon-fashion. A lot of what we'd now call old-fashioned roses were frantically vigorous, and one way to keep control and also make them flower better was by arching the long stems out all around the plants to form a star shape, and pegging the ends down. It looks attractive, and stops you getting snagged when you're weeding round them.

Plant-breeding produced endless new varieties, some good and some not so good. Really garden-worthy yellow roses appeared only after about 1880. The rose expert of the time was the Rev. Samuel Reynolds Hole, who wrote a number of very readable, if slightly eccentric, books on roses – but then, that's half the charm of Victorian authors. He wrote for William Robinson in *The Garden* magazine, and was the brains behind the National Rose Society, which was founded in 1876 and later became 'Royal'.

Shirley Hibberd

James Shirley Hibberd (1825–90) was a Victorian gardening writer from Muswell Hill, and author of Rustic Adornments for Homes of Taste, *which was full of bright ideas for interior decorating with plants. He was always, strangely, known as Shirley.*

The Plant-hunters

ABOVE: *Robert Fortune was a widely travelled plant collector and brought many new varieties into Britain.*

William Lobb worked for Veitch's nurseries in Exeter. He did a lot of collecting in Chile; his finds included *Berberis darwinii*, *Desfontainea spinosa* and *Escallonia macrantha*. His brother collected orchids in Burma and Borneo; these were especially valuable, though collecting them was very dangerous due to hostile tribes and tropical diseases. John Veitch, the nursery-owner's son, also collected plants for the family firm. He based himself in Japan during the 1860s and introduced hundreds of highly commercial plants, including *Lilium auratum*, the gold-rayed lily of Japan, *Primula japonica* and Virginia creeper (*Parthenocissus tricuspidata*). The same firm later employed Ernest Wilson, whose speciality was collecting plants in China, and who consequently became known as 'Chinese' Wilson. The Veitch nursery was sold in 1914.

Robert Fortune trained as a gardener at the Botanic Gardens in Edinburgh before joining the RHS in London as a plant-collector. His first destination was China, where the Royal Horticultural Society sent him with a 'shopping list' for their garden at Chiswick. He was to look for good, garden-worthy hardy shrubs and new varieties of fruit trees, unless, of course, he happened to spot any decent orchids, which would be good money-spinners to help defray the £1,800 cost of his three-year stint in China. He introduced forsythia, winter jasmine, *Skimmia japonica*, *Jasminum nudiflorum*, *Mahonia japonica* and *Anemone japonica* – a popular plant in Chinese graveyards. Fortune later visited Japan, from which he introduced tree peonies, *Dicentra spectabilis*, *Cryptomeria japonica*, *Weigela florida* and all sorts of chrysanthemums.

PLANTING FASHIONS AND INNOVATIONS

New plants were the lifeblood of Victorian gardens. They poured into the country from plant-hunters who were sent out all over the world by institutions such as Kew and the Royal Horticultural Society, and by private nurseries.

To hold your head up in Victorian gardening circles, it was essential to grow the right plants.

Hardy ferns were cultivated in 'stumperies' – artfully arranged piles of dead tree stumps stacked in a shady spot.

Coloured and variegated plants of all sorts were popular – copper beech, variegated hollies such as 'Handsworth New Silver' and, for the conservatory, *Abutilon striatum* 'Thompsonii'.

Evergreens were very fashionable, the gloomier the better. Portuguese laurels (*Prunus lusitanica*), spotted laurel (*Aucuba japonica*) and ivies as well as the

wide-leaved Japanese privet (*Ligustrum ovalifolium*), star of a million suburban hedges, and a lot of other newly arrived oriental evergreens, were popular – as much as anything because they didn't expire the minute they acquired a patina of soot. A secondary benefit was that they were cheaper to maintain than flowers, and labour costs were rising fast. Rhododendrons were especially collectable and in Cornwall, where the climate and acid soil were particularly suitable for them, large landowners re-created Himalayan ravines packed with 'rhodies'. Several of them are still there today. Glendurgan and Trebah are good examples of the 'Cornish Himalayas', and there's a very realistic Victorian ravine-style garden at the Lost Gardens of Heligan, near St Austell.

Large, weird plants that stood out were popular 'conceits' (which roughly translates as Victorian for 'eccentricities'). Tree ferns, if you lived in Cornwall, Wellingtonia – famous for being huge – Monkey puzzle and Gunnera. Of these, the Monkey puzzle tree most captured the imagination.

Archibald Menzies had first brought back seeds of the tree in 1795. He was the botanist/surgeon on a survey expedition to South America and Monkey puzzle nuts were served at the end of the dinner given by the governor of Chile. Curious, Menzies put a few in his pocket to grow later.

But it wasn't till William Lobb, who collected for Veitch's nurseries in Exeter brought back large quantities from Chile that the trees became affordable and widely available. (Lobb was also responsible for the great Victorian Wellingtonia craze, as he found a bulk source of seed in California.)

Thanks to their bizarre appearance, Monkey puzzles were soon the things to have. At Biddulph Grange young trees were used as 'dot' plants in bedding-out schemes, and they were later taken up as centrepieces of front gardens in suburban villas. They would become a problem a century or so later when they grew to an enormous size, but as yet there was no indication that they would develop the habit of unexpectedly shedding large branches on top of parked cars.

ABOVE: *Glendurgan in Cornwall is a stunning Victorian ravine-style garden.*

Upper-class plants

A collection of rare new plants was a great status symbol for the upper classes. But new plants weren't left long in the hands of the rich. By now nurseries were poised to propagate and distribute new 'finds' at affordable prices, and the plants were immediately pounced on by the social-climbing middle classes.

The emerging Royal Horticultural Society

One of the big gardening landmarks of Victoria's reign was the Horticultural Society becoming 'Royal'. It began life in a room over Hatchard's book shop in Piccadilly on 7 March 1804, where a consortium of gardening movers and shakers, including Sir Joseph Banks, Andrew Knight and John Wedgwood (son of Josiah, head of the famous pottery family), met to float the idea of a society 'for the advancement of gardening'. The Horticultural Society of London was the result.

The society began well. It leased 33 acres of ground at Chiswick from the Duke of Devonshire (its first President) for its official garden. It had offices in London, and started gathering together a library of horticultural books and prints.

Several plant-collectors were sent out, especially briefed to bring back good garden-worthy species. One of these collectors was David Douglas, who'd been recommended for the job by William Hooker. He introduced *Mahonia aquifolium*, *Limnanthes douglasii* (poached egg flower) and *Ribes sanguineum* (flowering currant), though he's better known for large conifers, such as the Douglas fir (*Pseudotsuga menziesii*), western red cedar (*Thuja plicata*)and sitka spruce (*Picea sitchensis*). Unfortunately, he came to a sticky end on a plant-hunting trip to Hawaii in 1834, when he fell into a concealed pit that the Hawaiians used as an animal trap, and found it was already occupied by a wild bull which gored him to death.

Prince Albert took over as president in 1858 after the Duke of Devonshire died, and in 1861 Queen Victoria decreed the society 'Royal'. The RHS was born. That same year the society opened a new garden in Kensington (right) on land previously used for the Great Exhibition, which had been shifted to south London.

Things were not looking so bright by 1882, however. Running two gardens was proving very expensive, and cash flow was giving serious cause for concern. In an effort to increase its appeal, the society mistakenly 'dumbed down' by providing amusements in its Kensington garden – which predictably didn't go down well with its stuffier members. It also had competition from the Botanical Society, which had started up in 1839. That society's garden at Regent's Park was drawing big crowds of visitors.

But the RHS did some refinancing, the Kensington garden lease wasn't renewed, economies were made and the tricky moment passed.

Things looked up in the society's centenary year, 1904, shortly after Victoria's death, when a benefactor made it possible for the society to acquire new premises in Vincent Square, which is still the RHS headquarters today. At the same time Sir Thomas Hanbury made the society a gift of 'Oakwood', a woodland garden near Ripley in Surrey. It had originally been owned by George Wilson, who'd made his fortune from Price's Patent Candles and spent the last 25 years of his life developing the garden to house his collection of exhibition lilies. This was phase one of the RHS gardens at Wisley. Things have steadily looked up.

ABOVE: In 1840 Kew became
a government organization
and opened to the public.

Genetics in plants

*Gregor Mendel's work
with tall and dwarf peas
between 1856 and 1874
made it possible to predict
which parent plants
would pass on desired
characteristics.
Previously, new plant
varieties were created by
hit-and-miss methods
without understanding
the 'rules' of inheritance
of plant characteristics.
It paved the way for
modern plant-breeding,
and today's F1 hybrids.*

KEW MAKES A COMEBACK

Kew Gardens had been largely left to go to seed since
the deaths of Sir Joseph Banks and George III, but in
1838, when the royal palaces and gardens were put
into public ownership, the committee involved
decided the fate of Kew. Their recommendation was
to put some real muscle behind it and put it to work
for the empire. In 1841 it became a government
organization, with William Hooker, former Professor
of Botany at Glasgow University, as its new director.

The first thing Hooker did was tidy the place up
and open it to the public. At first only part of the
grounds was opened, on weekday afternoons. It was
a huge success, and in the first year 9,000 visitors
came to Kew. Hooker commissioned an elaborate
palm house from Decimus Burton, which was built
between 1844 and 1848. It measured 363 x 100ft,
with a spiral staircase up to a walkway round the
inside of the roof, and cost £30,000. It was a huge
attraction. Palms became must-have Victorian
house-plants, and Burton went on to build the
temperate house at Kew.

To cope with the growing crowds the garden
began opening on Sunday afternoons as well, and by
the end of Victoria's reign Kew was drawing over a
million visitors each year. But they had to mind their
Ps and Qs. Smoking wasn't allowed, nor was
picnicking, or walking on patches of grass that were
designated 'keep off'. There was also a big problem
with people picking flowers – a ten-year-old girl was
actually put in prison overnight for doing so.

Kew also began sending out plant-hunters again.
One of the first was Hooker's son, Joseph. His
expeditions to the Himalayas between 1848 and 1851
brought back 28 new species of rhododendron, and
started a craze for them that swept the country. In
1871, the writer Shirley Hibberd claimed that 'the
money spent on rhododendrons during the past
20 years would pay off the national debt'. It was
certainly good news for the nursery trade.

Joseph took over his father's job as director of
Kew in 1865 and became one of the top botanists of
the century; for a time he was President of the Royal
Society. At Kew, Hooker Junior's big ambition was to
collect, study and classify the many thousands of

plants from all over the empire – a huge project that spawned several massive multivolume floras describing the plant life of places such as Australia and South Africa. The scientific area at Kew gradually increased from Augusta's original nine acres up to 150 acres.

But Kew's real forte was economic botany. One of its reasons for existence was to help obtain plants with industrial potential from their countries of origin, propagate them in bulk and transfer them to British colonies with the right growing conditions. There they'd be planted on plantation scale, to pump out the raw materials for goods that would create new jobs, open up new trade and generate a fat profit for the empire.

It worked. Thanks to Kew, rubber plants from the Amazon were introduced to Malaya, the quinine-yielding cinchona tree went to India, cotton was moved from the Sudan to India, coffee went to Africa, and bananas, sugar cane and pineapples to Jamaica. What had once been a very exclusive and expensive royal hobby helped Britain to become a superpower.

KEW SUCCESS STORIES

Quinine
One of the biggest killers in history – malaria – was already widespread throughout much of the British Empire, and the powers that be were keen to expand into new colonies in Africa, which were heavily infested with the disease. Thus, a cheap, reliable supply of quinine was essential – but it came only from the bark of the cinchona tree, which grew exclusively in South America, and it was illegal to remove live plants or seeds. In 1861 William Hooker sent out several collectors who managed to obtain stocks by bribing the locals. As a result, huge batches of cinchona plants were raised in the greenhouses at Kew and shipped out to the plantations of India.

Rubber
It was the Amazonian Indians who first discovered how to smoke the gooey sap from a local tree, *Hevea brasiliensis*, turning it into a tough, flexible material from which they made shoes and other useful objects. This started the rubber industry, which was a nice little earner for the government of Brazil, but, having a stranglehold on the world's supplies, they weren't keen to let anyone else in on the act. A Kew expert was called in to smuggle out some seeds. Speed was of the essence, since rubber tree seeds are viable only for a short time, but he managed to get a large shipment whizzed back to Kew. Within two weeks, the first seedlings came up, and young rubber plants were soon being sent out to Ceylon (now Sri Lanka) and Malaysia. By 1880 Britain had its own booming rubber business.

BELOW: The Victorians made use of the Amazonian Indians' discovery that the sap from Hevea brasiliensis *trees could produce rubber. They began to grow them in glasshouses like this one at Kew.*

Wardian Cases

ABOVE: *Nathaniel Ward revolutionized the transportation of plants for generations of plant collectors. The structure of the Wardian Cases (below) protected plants from the drying winds and salt air on sea voyages.*

The Wardian case was like a cross between a greenhouse and a suitcase. It was invented quite by accident in the 1830s when an amateur naturalist, Dr Nathaniel Ward, put a butterfly chrysalis into a glass jar to hatch, along with a handful of soil. When some weed seedlings came up he observed that they grew much better than similar seedlings in the open air on the window sill inside his room. The difference was due to air quality: the open air was too dry for the plants to flourish. He experimented by growing other plants under glass covers, and his cases became very fashionable for indoor gardening, particularly for ferns and other lovers of high humidity. Similar cases were also used for transporting plants on long sea voyages. By protecting the plants from drying winds, salt air and dehydration, the survival rate went up from a feeble 5 per cent to a whopping 95 per cent, and more plants could be shipped at a time because the cases could be strapped to the decks rather than kept below, where conditions were too dark. By making bulk plant transfers so successful, the Wardian case helped make Britain great.

NEW VICTORIAN GARDENS

From 1850 onwards Albert's heath started to deteriorate, and shortly before Christmas 1861 he died of typhoid fever. Victoria immediately went into deep mourning and shut herself away at Osborne House. She couldn't even bring herself to go to the funeral, and just sent flowers – violets and one early camellia that she picked in the gardens. She totally dropped out of public and private life, and all work on the houses and gardens came to a stop, apart from the most basic maintenance – even pruning wasn't allowed. Everything was left exactly as it was when Albert died: his gardens became, quite literally, a shrine to his memory.

At Frogmore Victoria had a huge and very grand Roman-style stone mausoleum with a copper roof built in the garden, inside which lay two matching white marble tombs. She wanted to be buried alongside her husband, which was a complete break from the normal royal funeral arrangements as kings and queens were normally buried in the chapel at Windsor.

After two years Victoria was reluctantly persuaded to resume some of her royal duties, but she rarely appeared in public again until the late 1870s – almost at the end of her reign. When she was at Windsor she would take her work out into the grounds at Frogmore, in order to feel close to Albert's mortal remains.

Buckingham Palace was virtually shut up after Albert's death, and 20 years later his room was still exactly as he'd left it. But if life stood still for Queen Victoria, out in Victorian gardens new momentum was gathering.

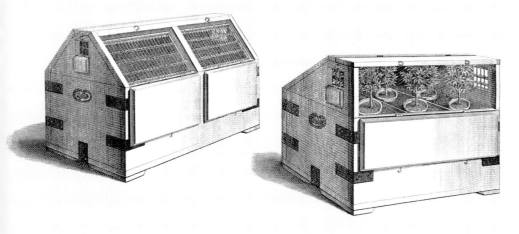

The 'Real Gardens' Movement

Towards the 1880s people were feeling a bit fed up with loud bedding and formal flower gardens, and the mood was right for a change. A more natural style of gardens began to evolve. William Robinson is credited with starting the ball rolling, though he might just have struck lucky, being in the right place with the right idea at the right time. The likes of Gertrude Jekyll, John Ruskin and William Morris went one step further and set out to recapture a complete 'lost' way of life by bringing back 'olde worlde' flower gardens, vernacular architecture, and distinctly rustic handmade craftsmanship after years of Victorian mass-produced stuff.

William Robinson

William Robinson's career began in Ireland, working in a clergyman's garden, where he was in charge of the glasshouses. One midwinter's day he walked out – and one is bound to suspect that he had fallen out with his employer in a big way because he quite deliberately shut down the boiler fires and opened all the ventilators. The plants were stone dead by morning.

He took himself off to London, where his past seems not to have caught up with him as he found a job with the Royal Botanic Society at Regent's Park. He stayed for eight years. It was there that he 'discovered' his special gardening interests – wild flowers and alpines.

ABOVE: William Robinson created his own gardens at Gravetye Manor, which is now a hotel where guests can enjoy the restored gardens.

INVENTION, INTRODUCTIONS AND INGENUITY

ABOVE: Gertrude Jekyll loved to create soft planting schemes to offset the hard landscaping designed by her partner, Edwin Lutyens. Upton Grey, Hampshire, is a beautifully restored example of her craft.

An early advocate of the natural style that's right back in fashion today, Robinson thought plants should come first and architecture last, or not at all – he had no time for what he termed 'pasty-work gardening'. His style was very much wild-flower meadows, naturalized bulbs and multistorey, cottage-garden-style planting schemes with no bare soil showing. He'd feel right at home today. One of his favourite planting associations was for rose beds carpeted with violets, pansies or thymes.

William Robinson's own garden was at Gravetye Manor, near East Grinstead, Sussex, and the house is now a very smart hotel and restaurant. The garden, which is open only to guests, has been restored in the Robinson style, with wild-flower meadows, lake and woods and is not far from Ingwersen's famous alpine plant nursery, which sits on what was once part of Robinson's 200-acre estate.

A prolific writer, Robinson is best known for the great natural gardening classic *The English Flower*

Garden, first published in 1883, but he also wrote about alpine flowers, subtropical plants and even cemetery gardens. He edited the English translation of Vilmorin-Andrieux's *The Vegetable Garden*, which gives a remarkable insight into the weird and wonderful vegetables available to Victorian gardeners. He also started a weekly magazine, *The Garden,* using many now-distinguished names as his contributors – it was William Robinson who 'discovered' Gertrude Jekyll.

Gertrude Jekyll

A professional artist, keen on rural crafts, Gertrude Jekyll took up gardening in later life when her eyesight became too bad for 'close work', despite thick glasses. Soon after meeting William Robinson in 1875 she started writing articles for his magazine, *The Garden*, and went on to write a number of books. She liked cottage-style gardens, and began her garden-design career by laying out one for her mother. By 1880 she was 'doing' gardens for other people. She brought an artist's eye to bear on her flowerbeds, and used hot or cool colours to create a 'mood'. Her pet hate was seeing blue and purple next to each other, and she'd often use them at opposite ends of the border with all the hot colours grouped together in the middle – a deliberate visual 'trick' to make a border look bigger. It also prevented potentially clashing colours being put next to each other. The best-known of her many books was *Colour in the Flower Garden.*

Jekyll often worked hand in glove with the architect Edwin Lutyens, the designer of New Delhi. They first met in 1889 and when, in 1897 Lutyens designed her house, Munstead Wood, Jekyll planned a soft, blowsy planting scheme to offset all the hard landscaping he'd put into the garden. His trademark style was to make 'garden rooms' with angular architectural details; while hers was to 'blur' these hard edges with a soft fringe of plants, such as hostas or hardy ferns, so that they melted into the landscape. The pair used the same winning formula in over a hundred gardens. Some of Jekyll's gardens have recently been restored to their original design, and one of the best examples is the Manor House at Upton Grey in Hampshire.

Pioneers of Arts and Crafts

William Morris didn't just design flowery wallpaper. He founded the Society for the Protection of Ancient Buildings, which eventually evolved into the National Trust we know today.

John Ruskin was a social commentator, artist and critic, who famously described the newfangled Crystal Palace as 'a cucumber frame'.

VICTORIAN COTTAGE GARDENS

At the very bottom of the ladder, however, the countryside wasn't sharing the great Victorian boom. Agricultural communities weren't doing well at all, and villages were in decline. Cottage gardens weren't the romantic 'roses round the door and hollyhocks at the gate' idyll you might think. 'Townies', whose families had long since left the land, had romantic notions of country life based on sentimental Victorian novels and watercolours. Real life was hens, pigs, cabbages and the odd patch of flowers, mostly throw-outs from the 'big house'. Unfashionable old plants ended up in cottage gardens – which is just as well. They were looked after, so when they made a comeback a century and a half later there were still a few left.

Today's chocolate-box cottage gardens are a romanticized version of the real thing, built up with layers of influence from the likes of William Robinson, Gertrude Jekyll and, later, Vita Sackville-West at her garden in Sissinghurst, Kent. But then, gardens and romance have always been inextricably entwined

THE END OF AN ERA

It took nearly 20 years and the influence of John Brown, the ghillie at Balmoral, to persuade Queen Victoria to start going out into the world again. In 1886 she started holding outdoor receptions at Buckingham Palace that would later evolve into the

OPPOSITE: *Osborne House was a favourite residence of the Queen, and a fitting place for her to spend her last years.*

famous garden parties. But, indoors, Albert's room was still untouched.

On the morning of her golden jubilee, Victoria had breakfast in the garden at Frogmore then travelled to London for the festivities, which ended at Buckingham Palace with fireworks in the garden.

Queen Victoria died at Osborne House on 22 January 1901, having overseen perhaps one of the most exciting gardening times ever.

ABOVE: *Inseparable in life and death, Victoria was laid to rest next to Albert in a specially built mausoleum at Frogmore.*

TWENTIETH-CENTURY GROWTH

**HOUSE OF SAXE-
COBURG-GOTHA**

Edward VII 1901–10

HOUSE OF WINDSOR

George V 1910–36
Edward VIII Jan–Dec 1936
George VI 1936–52
Elizabeth II 1952–

*OPPOSITE ABOVE: The
twentieth century brought
gardening passion to the
masses.*

*OPPOSITE BELOW:
Sandringham was a new
residence for the twentieth-
century royals, and one
whose garden was designed
to look good in winter when
it was most in use.*

By his late teens Victoria and Albert's eldest son, Edward (known in the family as 'Bertie'), was preoccupied with horse racing and unsuitable women. There had already been a bit of trouble over an actress – all most unbecoming in the future heir to the throne, especially considering Queen Victoria's big thing about moral standards.

After mulling over the problem, Edward's parents decided that it was high time he had some family responsibilities. They looked out for a royal wife, and came up with a very beautiful and gentle Danish princess, Alexandra. They also found the ideal country estate, Sandringham, an eighteenth-century house surrounded by 100 acres of woodland near King's Lynn in Norfolk, well away from the temptations of London, which they bought for his 21st birthday present.

SANDRINGHAM

The house was done up, and Edward moved in just in time for his wedding, in 1863. He gave the last-century landscape gardens a fashionable new 'natural look' along William Robinson lines – the perfect style for a house way out in the woods.

Although most royal country homes were used as summer holiday retreats, Sandringham was used mostly in winter since Edward liked to hold huge shooting parties, so great efforts were made to make the garden look its best when the couple were 'at home' entertaining.

Winter pansies were planted in beds where they could be seen from the drawing room windows, and there was an 'Italian Garden' where variegated evergreens were planted out temporarily, along with spring bulbs; winter bedding as we know it today wasn't available.

More trees were put in to brighten up the existing woodland, particularly Alexandra's favourites – Japanese maples – whose bright autumn colours were timed just right for the start of the shooting season. Rivulets of spring bulbs were planted, along with some huge herbaceous borders running off through clearings between the trees, which was a typical Robinsonian touch.

The formal 'landscaped' lake behind the house was filled in, and a big new natural-style water garden was made way out in the grounds, with three ornamental lakes connected by a series of streams and cascades. On a promontory jutting out into one of the lakes was a huge rock garden made from Pulhamite, the Victorian artificial stone. Considering how outrageous a lot of the rockeries of Victorian landowning eccentrics could be, this one was remarkably restrained. It was relatively level, more like a stone 'pavement', with the rock arranged in natural-ish strata, with a summer-house perched just behind it. The lakes were stocked with water lilies and waterside plants to complete the naturalizing process.

Since Sandringham was such a long way from the nearest town a well-stocked kitchen garden was a must, given all the entertaining that was done at the house. Edward started a small vegetable patch across the road from the house soon after he and Alexandra moved in, then, in 1896, he had a bit of luck on the horses and invested his winnings on enlarging the garden.

OPPOSITE: *Sandringham has a stunning mix of formal beds and abundant borders as well as its own vegetable garden.*

RIGHT: *Sandringham was carefully landscaped to provide beautiful views from the house.*

The result was a spectacular walled kitchen garden. It was surrounded by a high wall for growing trained fruit trees, and the centre was divided into quarters by paths that crossed at a fountain in the middle. The paths were outlined by impressive herbaceous borders that screened off the vegetables growing in neat and productive rows behind them. This 'look' was copied at upwardly mobile country houses all over the country, where a well-stocked and flower-lined formal kitchen garden became a great status symbol to be shown off to envious house guests during the regulation Sunday afternoon tour of the grounds.

The Sandringham kitchen garden was very productive as it had to cater for huge numbers of 'society' guests, all bringing their own personal servants; it wasn't unusual to have over 100 extra mouths to feed. But because winter was the peak entertaining season, out-of-season crops were a speciality at Sandringham. There was a large apple store to 'keep' fruit harvested from the kitchen garden walls, and forcing pits were used to produce early and late crops of vegetables and salads. Winter vegetables were grown in serious quantities for dinner parties, and a whole acre of celery was grown, just to provide 'sticks' for guests to nibble with their cheese at the end of a meal.

Glasshouses were provided to raise all the fashionable pot plants needed for the house. Poinsettias had only just been introduced, Malmaison carnations and gardenias were grown for buttonholes, and lily of the valley was forced for winter table decorations.

Not long before Victoria died 'Arts and Crafts' touches began to creep into the garden at

Sandringham. A long pergola was added for fragrant climbing roses and honeysuckle, with wide borders for pillar roses, creating the romantic 'look' that nowadays we think of as typical of an Edwardian flower garden.

For someone who was clearly bent on a playboy lifestyle, it might seem surprising to find that Edward was such a keen gardener – but, then, he'd started young. As a child he'd spent the summer at Osborne House, where, along with the rest of Victoria and Albert's family, gardening had been firmly on the menu. In later life, he said if he hadn't been king, he'd have liked to be a gardener.

Edward's London home was Marlborough House, and it was here that Princess Alexandra started a new trend in indoor floral decorations. Instead of typically Victorian displays of potted plants sunk in banks of moss she arranged leafy tree branches in big vases, which was considered very forward-looking at the time. Cut flowers had hardly started to make their mark, except as dinner-table decorations and buttonholes.

But the ethereal Alexandra didn't really fit in with Edward's racy lifestyle, and as she was growing rather deaf, she made her excuses and spent more time at Sandringham, where she loved the garden, and diplomatically ignored her husband's string of mistresses. It went with the job.

Country house parties

The wealthy offspring of successful Victorians had swelled the ranks of the country house-owning classes. Well-off families had little to do except entertain, and weekend parties provided entry into fashionable society. (This was the era of P. G. Wodehouse's tales of Bertie Wooster and his 'gentleman's gentleman', Jeeves.) A certain amount of licence was allowed, and the Edwardian speciality of romantic flower gardens must have provided a conducive atmosphere.

LATE BEGINNINGS

Due to his mother's exceptionally long reign, Edward didn't inherit the throne until he was 60. He reluctantly moved to Buckingham Palace, which was cluttered with Victoria's memorabilia – and Albert's room had still never been touched, half a century after his death. The first thing he did was to have a big clear-out. Once he'd smartened the place up he carried on the tradition of holding garden parties that Victoria had started towards the end of her life. But after waiting so long in the wings, Edward only lived to be king for nine years.

To celebrate Edward VII's coronation the island of Jersey held its first Battle of Flowers. Participants built wooden floats in the shape of fairy-tale castles, carriages or historical scenes, and covered them with fresh flowerheads. They were hitched up to horses and paraded through the main street of the island's capital, St Helier, where onlookers tore the flowers off and pelted each other with petals – hence the parade's name.

The Battle of Flowers has since become a regular event and is a favourite with late-summer tourists, though it's a tad more genteel nowadays. Today the floats are built on the backs of slow-moving lorries; the displays are put on show rather than stripped of their flowers and there's no 'fight' afterwards. Visitors can enjoy the spectacle in peace as the street is closed to traffic; stands are put up and you can even book seats in advance.

Edward's successor George V, and his wife Queen Mary, both loved Sandringham and moved into a cottage in the grounds so that Alexandra could stay in the main house, which had been her home for

years. Their youngest son, Prince John, who suffered badly from epilepsy and was rarely seen in public, lived almost permanently at Sandringham with a nurse until his early death.

When George had to be in London he stayed at Buckingham Palace, where, being a man of regular habits, he always went for a walk around the garden every day before lunch. But it was more for the good of his health than from any interest in gardening. (His big passion was stamp collecting.) Despite that, he always wore a gardenia in his buttonhole, and had a fresh one every day. One of the royal duties he bitterly loathed was the compulsory royal tour of the Chelsea Flower Show, and he always insisted on being taken round by the quickest possible route.

THE CHELSEA FLOWER SHOW

The Royal Horticultural Society had been holding regular flower shows under canvas at its Chiswick gardens between 1837 and 1883. The following year it decided to hold a bigger two-day spring show in the inner sanctum of the legal profession, the Temple Gardens. This became an annual event until 1911, when the lawyers took umbrage at the rowdy crowds and the mess they left behind. They made such a fuss that the RHS thought it time to look for another venue.

It settled on Chelsea, where a very successful horticultural exhibition had been held by someone else in 1912. The RHS promptly ordered itself a big new marquee, and its next spring show was held in the grounds of the Royal Hospital, where it's still staged today.

LEFT: *By 1914 the RHS Flower Show had moved to its current venue in the grounds of the Royal Hospital, giving birth to what we now know as the Chelsea Flower Show.*

The old marquee

Chelsea visitors had a soft spot for the 'old marquee'. In fact, it wasn't always the same one. Canvas yellows with age, which 'tints' the light and stops visitors seeing the true colours of the flowers, so the 'old marquee' was actually a series of identical models that were replaced every 12 years. After its final outing, the 'old marquee' was sent off for recycling, and the canvas was made into gardening aprons, tote bags and other mementos, which were sold at the show.

It wasn't that much different from the Chelsea Flower Show we know now except that the judges all wore bowler hats, and the visitors were mainly the landed gentry with their deferential head gardeners in tow.

In those early years the big trend for outdoor gardens was rockeries, which were all the rage at the time, and in the marquee upmarket plants, such as orchids and stovehouse exotics, featured heavily. A few of the exhibitors were firms you still see showing at Chelsea today, including Notcutts Nurseries, with their superb displays of shrubs, and the begonia specialists Blackmore & Langdon.

Due to wartime difficulties the show wasn't put on at all in 1918. When it came back the following year Queen Alexandra visited on the first day. This set the seal of approval on Chelsea, the royal visit became a regular fixture, and for debutantes 'coming out' a day at the famous flower show became an essential part of the London season.

Despite the fact that George V wasn't a gardening fan, and neither was he terribly keen on being frogmarched round the show, he went – under pressure. He got very grumpy if press photographers harassed him. His chief interest was the vegetable displays, and in 1924 an exhibitor whose stand he'd admired at a previous show added 'King George' cucumbers to his arrangement specially to attract the royal eye. The same year, the King spotted some aubergines on a stand at the show and asked for a few samples to be sent across to the palace for tasting.

His eldest son and heir, Prince Edward, on the other hand, was very keen on his visits to Chelsea, and in 1934 he bought up a complete exhibit – a rock garden – when the show was over, and had it put in his garden at Fort Belvedere, his imitation castle near Windsor.

Chelsea wasn't staged at all during the Second World War and started up again only in 1947, when rhododendrons were the 'plant of the moment'. For the first time, a reigning monarch actually took part in the show instead of just visiting: George IV entered a display of schizanthus from the royal greenhouses.

RIGHT: *The Chelsea Flower Show has long enjoyed visits by the royal family – George VI and his queen were regular visitors.*

A gala occasion

Nowadays the royal party visits the show on press day – the Monday of Chelsea week. The showground is cleared at 3.30 p.m. so that its members can go round with only a small, select party of RHS minders, TV crews and journalists. After they have left, as dusk gathers, a charity gala is held when smartly dressed party-goers preview the show with a glass of champagne and canapés. Tickets for the gala sell out long in advance, and the proceeds go to good causes.

Schizanthus, also known as poor man's orchid, is something you don't see grown much these days; it's a wonderful annual winter or spring pot-plant, brilliant for cool conservatories.

The show grew steadily. Nearly all the exhibitors were nurseries, who either built outdoor gardens or staged displays of plants in the marquee. One thing they weren't allowed to do was sell plants – visitors had to place an order with the firm's representative on the stand, for delivery later.

It wasn't until the early 1970s that garden designers really started to make their mark at Chelsea. From then on, the show became much more 'ideas' oriented rather than purely practical. As head gardeners were by now much thinner on the ground more of the general public came in, there was more media coverage and 'designer gardens' took off. But well-dressed society ladies were still very much in evidence, complete with serious outfits, hats and high-heeled shoes. When the showground turned into a sea of mud after a sudden downpour, they'd show true breeding by stepping into plastic carrier bags, tying them round their ankles and carrying on as usual.

The show continued to attract more visitors until, at peak times, the grounds were dangerously overcrowded. The final straw came in 1987, when a quarter of a million visitors were packed in like sardines, and the queues for the ladies loos stretched halfway across the show.

The RHS considered moving to a bigger site outside London but by now the grounds of the Royal Hospital, and its colourful Chelsea Pensioners in their red uniforms, were part of the tradition. So instead of moving it restricted the number of visitors by half. It also kept the first two days of the show for RHS members only, and instead of sending them a free Chelsea ticket as part of their membership package, they made them pay. Naturally, there were howls of protest, but it worked, and the RHS signed up twice as many members as it lost.

In millennium year the old cotton-duck marquee, which had been on its last legs for a while, was replaced by a pair of modern steel and white PVC pavilions with roofs that could only have been inspired by ice-cream cones. They are better ventilated, which keeps the floral displays cooler, and, as a bonus, the gap between the two structures opens up a view of the frontage of Wren's magnificent Royal Hospital, which had always been hidden by the old marquee.

Chelsea may no longer signal the start of the debs' London season, but for some time it has been the place to spot emerging gardening trends. It's the international shop window for talented garden designers, and the springboard for new plant varieties – especially roses – to be launched to the public. In gardening terms, it has always been the greatest show on Earth.

WHO'S WHO OF EDWARDIAN GARDENERS

Miss Ellen Willmott, 1858–1934
A keen flower photographer, gardener and gardening writer, who swapped seeds with enthusiasts all over the world; she was a great friend of Gertrude Jekyll. Ellen Willmott had gardens in France and Italy, as well as her most famous one, Warley Place in Essex, and is reputed to have employed 103 gardeners. She is best known today for the plant that is named after her – 'Miss Willmott's Ghost' (*Eryngium giganteum*), a reference to her habit of sprinkling its seeds in the gardens she visited, so it followed in her wake a year later.

Edward Augustus Bowles, 1865–1954
Always known as E.A. Bowles; the epitome of the perfect English gent, whose home was Myddleton House, Enfield, London. Forced to abandon plans to become a clergyman, E.A. stayed at home and managed the garden, turning an old quarry into a pond and adding new plants, particularly bulbs, and a 'lunatic asylum' of peculiar plants, such as the curly corkscrew hazel, to what by all accounts were originally rather gloomy grounds. He became an expert on crocuses, snowdrops and colchicums, and is best known for the trio of seasonal gardening books he wrote – *My Garden in Spring*, *My Garden in Summer* and *My Garden in Autumn* – which are classics of gardening literature.

Lawrence Johnston, 1871–1958
The naturalised American creator of Hidcote Manor (right), near Chipping Campden, Gloucestershire, which he laid out from 1907 onwards. He famously divided the area up into a series of hedged garden 'rooms', each with its own character, the most famous of which is the Red Garden. Major Johnston was a great plantsman with a strong sense of design, and Hidcote has been the inspiration for a good many other well-known gardeners, including Vita Sackville-West at Sissinghurst. Hidcote was taken over by the National Trust in 1948.

Vita Sackville-West, 1892–1962
While her husband travelled the world as a diplomat, Vita Sackville-West stayed at home at Sissinghurst, Kent, gardening. Her famous gardening books and newspaper columns were written in a room at the top of the Elizabethan tower, where she could look down over the source of her inspiration. Sissinghurst is reckoned to contain just about every element of a fashionable Edwardian garden, and is famous for its White Garden, which contains hints of lilac with silver and grey foliage; Vita had a talent for picking winning plant associations, which are visible everywhere. Sissinghurst is now the National Trust's most heavily visited garden, so anticipate considerable overcrowding if you visit at weekends.

OPPOSITE: *The White Garden at Sissinghurst, in Kent is probably the best-known feature of Vita Sackville-West's popular garden.*

TWENTIETH-CENTURY GARDENING

The royal family had never found it necessary to worry much about its image before, but with the start of the First World War that had to change. It was PR or bust. When it picked up early warning signs that its Germanic surname, Saxe-Coburg-Gotha, sounded as if the family was on the Kaiser's side, it decided to change the name to something more patriotic. The King picked Windsor, after the residence with the longest history of any royal home, which stood for everything English.

Between 1914 and 1918, King George V and Queen Mary did their bit for the war effort by going out and about to meet their subjects. They visited hospitals, inspected the troops and opened the garden at Buckingham Palace to injured officers. And, just like 'normal' people, they started growing vegetables down the garden.

By the end of the war Edward, the heir to the throne, was running around with married women, so clearly it was high time he found a wife. As all the marriageable princesses were German and therefore out of bounds PR-wise, the search continued. Meanwhile, his younger brother, Prince Albert, Duke of York, married Lady Elizabeth Bowes-Lyon in 1923. She was a very sensible choice, a charming and good-looking girl from an old Scottish family. She'd been brought up at Glamis Castle in Forfar by a gardening mother, from whom she had inherited her 'feel' for flowers.

As Duke and Duchess of York, Albert and Elizabeth made their home at the Royal Lodge, Windsor. The house was by now in a shocking state so it was done up specially for them, and 15 acres of undergrowth around it were cleared to make a new garden. As gardening fans, they followed progress with interest.

The rising garden-design stars of the time were brought in. The landscape architect Geoffrey Jellicoe put in a terrace with steps down to the lawn, and his partner, Russell Page, arranged the planting schemes for a series of sunken gardens that were made all round the house.

Further away from the house, rhododendron walks were planted through the existing mature trees – all that was left of George IV's old landscape garden. The soil was naturally acid, and so rhododendrons were an obvious choice to plant; being cheap and easy to look after. This was the early

LEFT: *Wakehurst Place in West Sussex has a spectacular display of rhododendrons. It was planted in this style in the 1930s.*

Sunken gardens

Sunken gardens were to become popular features of fashionable gardens for years to come. As long as your soil was deep enough for there to be no risk of digging down into ghastly subsoil, they were also quite practical. A sunken garden was very sheltered, which was good for herbaceous plants, and made it pleasant to sit in, and it added a feeling of changing levels to the view from the house.

1930s, the Depression was in full swing and the royals didn't want to alienate public opinion by going in for conspicuous heavy spending.

Meanwhile, at nearby Fort Belvedere, the Duke's elder brother Edward was developing his own woodland-style rhododendron garden with the help of Eric Savill, the deputy surveyor of Windsor Great Park. He'd chosen the style as it reminded him of Sandringham, where he'd had so much fun as a child.

Rhododendrons and woodlands were the fashionable plant association between the wars for anyone with the right sort of soil. A number of now-famous gardens had been planted in much the same style around this time, including Exbury Gardens near Southampton in Hampshire, Bodnant at Colwyn Bay in Wales, and Leonardslee near Horsham and Wakehurst Place near Hayward's Heath, both in West Sussex. Naturally, acid soil was a 'must'. People on 'normal' ground who tried to follow the fashion were often disappointed. Even digging out beds and replacing the soil with peat didn't work for long: once the rhodies' roots spread to the surrounding soil the plants turned anaemic-looking and lost interest in life.

Around this time, Eric Savill began developing a piece of woodland about four miles from Windsor Castle. He underplanted the existing woodlands with rhododendrons, camellias and azaleas, and put in spectacular flowering trees, such as ornamental cherries, magnolias and the pocket handkerchief

Smith's Lawn

The polo ground that we know as Smith's Lawn, the stamping ground of the current Prince of Wales, sits halfway between the Savill Garden and Virginia Water. Before becoming a polo lawn it was used as a campsite for troops during the First World War, and later became a small airstrip for training RAF pilots on Tiger Moths.

Smith's Lawn is the home of the Guards Polo Club (president HRH Prince Philip), and they play from April to September.

tree, *Davidia involucrata*. Since the country was still suffering from post-war shortages, he had to scratch around for plants. When he learned that the primulas that were used for the spring bedding displays in St James's Park were thrown away afterwards, he managed to scrounge a truckload to replant at the Savill Garden, where he left them to naturalize and form big drifts.

George V and Queen Mary visited the new garden in spring 1934 and liked what they saw, but commented that it was a bit small, which gave Savill *carte blanche* to expand his ideas. He carried on the good work. Nowadays the Savill Garden is open to the public throughout the summer – it is at its most colourful in late spring and autumn.

By the time the Savill Garden was well under way, George V was in failing health. (He'd always been a heavy smoker.) In January 1936, after three months convalescing at a famous Sussex seaside town, he seemed somewhat better. But when his attendant tried to cheer him up, following a relapse, by suggesting that soon he'd be well enough to go back for another visit, it provoked the famously pithy last words, 'Bugger Bognor'.

George's eldest son became Edward VIII. He'd been groomed for the job all his life, but his heart wasn't really in it. One of his first royal duties was to clear the backlog of debutantes who hadn't been able to come out while his father too ill to receive them – in those days debs were still presented at court. So he threw a couple of large garden parties in the garden at Buckingham Palace, with 600 debs at each. To do the honours, Edward was seated under an exotic tent with silver poles brought back from an official visit to India by his parents. But he didn't make himself popular by clearing off early when it started to rain.

The problem was that he'd already met and fallen in love with the American Wallis Simpson, who had not only been divorced, but was still married to husband number two at the time Edward became king. He realized that she would be considered a most unsuitable royal wife, but he couldn't live without her. It was quite a quandary. Eleven months after coming to the throne, and just before his coronation, Edward abdicated.

As second in line, his brother Albert was automatically promoted to the spotlight. When he was crowned he took his father's name – he thought Albert sounded too German for post-war Britain – and the history books know him as George VI.

rationing during the Second
World War made the British
grow their own veg. Queen
Elizabeth visited land girls
in 1941, and her own
daughters, Elizabeth and
Margaret, mucked in with
the rest of the nation.

THE SECOND WORLD WAR

George VI and Queen Elizabeth moved into Buckingham Palace straight away. The gloomy Victorian shrubberies were cleared away and the garden was made much more family friendly. A swimming pool and squash courts were put in especially for the couple's two daughters, Princesses Elizabeth and Margaret.

The job was barely finished before the Second World War broke out. During one of the very first air raids on London a bomb fell through the roof of the squash court and blew the lot to smithereens. That incident produced the famous sound bite when Queen Elizabeth told a lady-in-waiting: 'I'm glad we've been bombed. Now I can look the East End in the face.'

Being such an easily recognizable landmark, Buckingham Palace was an easy target for Hitler's bombers, and the house and grounds took nine direct hits during the war. Although the children were sent off to Windsor for safety, the King and Queen Elizabeth lived there throughout the war, to show solidarity with Londoners.

But out in the royal gardens all the gardeners under 25 were called up. Big cutbacks had to be made. Flowerbeds were grassed over and lawns left uncut to reduce maintenance. Older staff were allowed to stay: as long as they were helping to grow vegetables, they were contributing to the nation's food supply. George VI and the queen threw themselves wholeheartedly into the Dig for Victory campaign.

Dig for Victory

With its fast-rising population Britain had not been self-sufficient in food for a long time, and relied heavily on imports. As the war began to bite, Hitler tried to starve the country into submission by sinking food-carrying convoys. Food rationing began on 8 January 1940.

Everybody was asked to do their bit for the war effort by producing as much food as they could at home. On 10 September 1940, the Dig for Victory campaign was launched. Mr Middleton, the radio

gardener, was asked to slip snippets of horticultural propaganda into his broadcasts. He was encouraged to persuade listeners to take on an allotment, and to grow winter vegetables, such as kale, leeks and sprouts, instead of just dabbling with the faster summer crops – after all, people needed to eat all year round.

The Ministry of Agriculture, in conjunction with the RHS, produced leaflets on vegetable-growing for beginners. Their *Vegetable Garden Displayed* was an instant best-seller and remained a classic well into the 1960s. Professional gardeners were asked to teach veg-growing to amateurs in their spare time, and the Women's Institute gave demonstrations of jam-making and fruit-bottling.

Within a year of war breaking out all sorts of essentials were hard to come by; powdered eggs and milk replaced the real thing, and Spam appeared on the menu. Besides growing vegetables, people were encouraged to feed kitchen and garden scraps to hens and rabbits, and to club together to rear a pig. A lot of bartering went on, with surplus garden produce being swapped for other things, and everything possible was recycled.

Potato-growing was heavily promoted, as spuds are filling and store well for winter. The cartoon

The Start of Media Gardening

Mr Middleton started the ball rolling in 1934 when he began broadcasting his 15-minute series *In Your Garden*, which went out on the BBC Home Service at 2.15 p.m. on Sunday afternoons. He soon had 3.5 million listeners. Gardening flowed in his veins – he was the son of a head gardener, and had worked in the seed trade before going to Kew as a student. When the BBC were looking for a radio gardener, the RHS recommended him, and by the time BBC TV started, Mr Middleton was the natural choice as gardening presenter. He was soon joined by Fred Streeter, the head gardener at Petworth Park in Sussex, and the genial Percy Thrower, superintendent of the parks department at Shrewsbury, who, earlier in his career, had worked in the royal gardens at Windsor. Percy's first-ever appearance on screen produced the offer of his very own series, *Gardening Club*. For the next 50 years, Percy was the face of gardening, appearing on everything from *Blue Peter* to *Gardeners' World*, until he crossed swords with the BBC over their no-advertising rule – and lost.

ABOVE: For 50 years, Percy Thrower was the face of gardening and helped stir up a passion for plants.

Windsor at war

'Farmer George', as George III was nicknamed, started a farm within Windsor Great Park, but after his death it had run down, and by Victorian times was once again a deer park. During the Second World War, however, it was revived to help the country's food supply. Most of the deer were culled, providing much-needed meat, and 2,000 extra acres of land were brought into cultivation. But a small breeding herd was kept to restock the deer park once the war was over.

character Potato Pete was created, along with his own recipe book. By 1941 a million acres of spuds were being grown. Carrots were used instead of sugar in all sorts of recipes, and parsnips could be cunningly disguised as bananas (which vanished from greengrocers' shops for years) by cooking them with golden syrup. To ward off vitamin deficiencies as a result of a diet of mainly bread and potatoes, the Ministry of Agriculture started the myth that carrots help you see in the dark. Nasturtium-leaf sandwiches were also recommended for their vitamin C content, which suggested that nasturtiums were good salad substitutes – they taste vile.

As the bombing grew heavier, Anderson shelters appeared in most back gardens. They were made by digging a big hole in the ground, roofing it with corrugated iron sheets and then throwing the soil back over the top to cushion the impact. The more pragmatic gardeners used their air-raid shelters for forcing rhubarb and mushrooms, and most people grew marrows over the roof. These were turned into a typically thrifty wartime 'delicacy' – mock goose – made by stuffing a giant marrow with a mixture of minced onion, herbs, cooking fat, breadcrumbs and any other leftovers in the back of the larder.

Smokers were allowed to grow tobacco as long as it was for their own use and not for sale. 'Smoking' tobacco (*Nicotiana tabacum*) looks like a giant version of our popular bedding tobacco plants, six feet tall but with narrow, tubular, pale-pink to reddish flowers. The huge oval leaves were picked in autumn as they were just turning yellow, then pegged out on the washing line to dry in the sun. They were finished off by being hung from strings

inside a shed. After being packed into thick wads and cured with molasses, they'd be shredded up ready to roll. Results were variable to say the least, and a lot of people started smoking home-grown herbal mixtures or dried blackberry leaves instead.

Glasshouses at big country estates and commercial nurseries were turned over to compulsory tomato production. Their high vitamin content made tomatoes a worthwhile food crop, while luxuries such as cucumbers and peaches were officially considered a waste of valuable resources. Specialist nurseries usually managed to reserve enough stock to get back into production after the war, but it would take time to build up supplies again.

National Growmore, the first-ever commercially manufactured general-purpose fertilizer appeared on sale, and householders were encouraged to save soot (for its nitrogen content and slug-deterrent powers) and use the manure from rabbits, chickens and pigs on the vegetable garden. Every little helped. People dug up their back lawns and flowerbeds to grow vegetables. One in five homes had an allotment, and between them they generated an estimated two million tons of extra food. Every scrap of spare land, including playing fields, the London parks, Spalding bulbfields and even Kensington Gardens, was ploughed up to grow food, and a piggery was started in Hyde Park.

With all the able-bodied men away fighting, girls were recruited to work on farms. The Land Army was made operational in 1939, and eventually there were 90,000 'land girls' turned out in fetching uniforms of khaki jodhpurs and sweaters.

Daylight saving was brought in and British Summer Time was continued right through the

winter. Then, in 1941, double summer time started so that factory workers could spend a couple of hours in their allotments after work. People had never worked so hard, but it was well worth the effort. Between 1939 and 1945 food imports were halved.

Post-war Renovations

By the end of the war, it's fair to say that the royal gardens were looking neglected and a lot of tidying up was needed. Gardeners were slowly trickling back to work, but men who'd learnt new trades in wartime weren't so keen on going back to their old jobs with low wages and long hours. Economy and low maintenance became the top priorities in post-war royal gardens.

At the Savill Garden, besides getting on top of the undergrowth, it was decided to add a new feature to give the garden a modern 'twist' – a wall for training tender shrubs. Since building materials were in very short supply it was built from old bricks rescued from London bomb-sites. It was also decided to go ahead with a big new project: the Valley Garden, between Smith's Lawn and Virginia Water. There the

plan was to bulk out the existing natural woodland with rhododendrons plus shrubs for autumn colour, fruit and berries, all planted naturalistically to suit the contours of the site. Since the project called for huge quantities of plants, which were also hard to find just after the war, a big new nursery was built specially to propagate them.

At Sandringham the garden was ripe for a gentle makeover, and now that there were more cars on the roads the drive leading to the house was becoming overlooked. The landscape architect Geoffrey Jellicoe was asked back. He re-routed the drive and redesigned that part of the garden with tall yew hedges, dividing the space up into 'rooms', which were planted by the famous landscape architect Sylvia Crowe. The work was still being done in 1952 when George VI died.

Princess Elizabeth was on a visit to Treetops Reserve in Kenya with her husband Prince Philip, Duke of Edinburgh, when the news of her father's death reached her. She returned home straight away. The couple then immediately moved into Buckingham Palace with their two children, Prince Charles and Princess Anne.

ABOVE: The Valley Garden in Windsor was one of the first royal gardening projects after the Second World War. It is planted with shrubs and rhododendrons to give long periods of colour in a natural setting.

OVERLEAF: Geoffrey Jellicoe redesigned part of the garden at Sandringham, separating the space into 'rooms' using high yew hedges.

*RIGHT: Queen Elizabeth
the Queen Mother, Prince
Charles and Princess Anne
at Windsor.*

*OPPOSITE: The walled garden
at the Castle of Mey, in
Caithness, north Scotland.
The Great Wall of Mey
surrounding the castle is
12 ft high and protects
the plants from salt spray
and severe gales.*

ELIZABETH II

Neither the Queen nor the Duke was particularly
expert at gardening. Other outdoor activities were
very much more their scene – riding and horse
racing for the Queen, shooting and carriage-driving
for the Duke. But the royal gardens had to be kept
up, with a tight rein on expenses. Flowerbeds were
replanted with low-maintenance, ground-cover
shrubs or else totally grassed over wherever
possible, and manpower-guzzling great greenhouses
and kitchen gardens became a thing of the past.

It wasn't only royalty who were feeling the pinch
– middle-class gardeners who had once employed a
jobbing gardener suddenly found themselves having
to manage without. Summer bedding, traditional
rosebeds and herbaceous borders were now too
much trouble, and people replanted their beds with
spreading ground-cover plants to smother out weeds
and provided year-round effect without much work.
The great heather and conifer craze followed soon
after – another time-saving style. But once 'designer
gardens' became fashionable people stopped seeing
gardening as a chore, and instead it became 'sexy'.
Soon the general public took over from royalty as the
innovative gardeners. With only pocket hanky-sized
gardens to look after, it was more practical to treat
yourself to a new look every few years.

The Queen Mother's Gardens

When Elizabeth II took the throne George VI's
widow, Queen Elizabeth the Queen Mother, moved
into Clarence House with her younger daughter,
Princess Margaret, and continued with her gardening.

Clarence House had only a small garden and,
to make matters worse, it was cast in deep shade all
summer by large, overhanging London plane trees.
But even if the gardening possibilities were limited,
it was very suitable for the Queen Mother's own
occasional garden parties.

At Windsor she continued to use the Royal Lodge,
though she didn't do anything new to the garden –
she liked it as it had been during the King's lifetime.
(He'd only recently removed a rockery from the
grounds – they were his big gardening 'hate', though
with his usual tact he kept quiet about it as he didn't
want to offend rock-garden fans.)

On the Balmoral estate in Scotland the Queen
Mother still had the use of Birkhall, a fairly
substantial white 'farmhouse' she and George VI
had used since they were first married. The garden
had a late-Victorian layout with large, atmospheric
drifts of herbaceous flowers planted specially for late
summer and early autumn colour, when they were
in residence. Being practical, there was no point in
having a garden that looked wonderful when no one
was there to enjoy it.

Eighty, not out

To celebrate the Queen Mother's 80th birthday, the royal parks created a 20-ft crown out of royal purple African violets at the Chelsea Flower Show, and the National Farmer's Union staged a crown of vegetables.

ABOVE AND RIGHT: The Queen Mother loved to grow brightly coloured plants in the glasshouses and borders around the Castle of Mey, and was especially fond of sweet peas.

In 1952 the Queen Mother bought the Castle of Mey, which was to be her own private house. As the most northerly castle in Britain, you'd think gardening here would be impossible. The castle is in a particularly exposed spot, right on the Caithness coast, six miles from John o'Groats and looking over to the Orkneys. But the Queen Mother took advantage of the only available shelter – an old walled kitchen garden – in which to make a series of garden 'rooms'. With stone walls outside, and hedges dividing the garden inside, there was enough protection from the elements to grow a colourful mixture of flowers, fruit and vegetables, which again were all chosen to be looking their best when she was on holiday there, in August and October. The Queen Mother liked feminine flowers in pastel pinks, blues and white, especially if they were scented – her real favourites were old-fashioned roses, sweet peas and lavender.

To safeguard its future, the Queen Mother turned the castle and its surrounding 2,000 acres of farmland into a Charitable Trust, with the Prince of Wales as its president. It's now open to the public from May to October.

RIGHT: *The lake at Buckingham Palace is surrounded by trees and informal planting.*

Elizabeth II as a gardener

Despite rumours to the contrary, the Queen is remarkably knowledgeable when it comes to gardening, as many a nurseryman at the Chelsea Flower Show has discovered. It might not be her number one pastime, but she knows the names of plants and flowers, and misses very little. She is not a fan of massive makeovers, and once remarked to me that some gardening being undertaken at Sandringham was 'not my kind of gardening'.

'What kind of gardening is that, ma'am?' I asked.

'The kind that uses a bulldozer,' she replied.

Buckingham Palace Garden Parties

At Buckingham Palace the basic outline of trees and shrubs that George IV had planted more than 100 years earlier had grown up, which was just as well. When London was rebuilt after the war, all the surrounding buildings were so much taller than before that a framework of mature trees was all that stood between the palace grounds and prying eyes.

For the interior of the garden, instead of the flowerbeds and formal features you might have expected, the space was developed as a low-maintenance wild garden. It's now virtually a giant nature reserve, which is refreshing to find right in the heart of London. The Queen has made a few small modifications; she's added a colourful laburnum tunnel, a rose garden and an avenue of horse chestnuts, and George IV's lake has had pink flamingos wading about in it.

But although Her Majesty regularly walks the corgis in the grounds when she's in residence, the garden is used mainly for entertaining on a grand scale.

George IV started the ball rolling, but his parties were a bit more disorderly than the genteel occasions they are nowadays. Royal garden parties as we know them were started by Queen Victoria, who received debutantes 'coming out' at two garden parties every summer. That tradition came to an end only in 1958, and now the Queen holds three garden parties each July, with guests chosen from a cross-section of the public.

The festivities start at 3 p.m., when the gates open. Everyone is ushered through the palace to the terrace and lawns behind it, where they can wander around the garden and listen to the band. At 4 p.m. the Queen joins her guests, talking briefly to as many people as possible while working her way down the garden towards the tea tent. Then, at 6 p.m. sharp, the band plays the national anthem as the signal for everyone to go home.

The show goes on whatever the weather. In 1996 one of the trees in the garden was stuck by lightning during a thunderstorm, but the tea and chatter just carried on as usual.

The biggest event ever held in the garden at Buckingham Palace was the party held for the Queen's golden jubilee in 2002, when a giant stage and banks of seats were put in for two huge concerts that were televised around the world, the first being a classical concert and the second a pop concert.

THE PRINCE OF WALES AND HIGHGROVE

As far as the current royal family is concerned, the keenest gardener of all is the Prince of Wales.

Prince Charles started gardening when he acquired his own garden at Highgrove, the eighteenth-century country mansion in Gloucestershire that was bought in 1981 by the Duchy of Cornwall and which the Prince rents.

When he took it on the house was surrounded by typically English parkland, with a few fine old trees and the 'shell' of an eighteenth-century walled vegetable garden, but nothing much else. It was the sort of big blank canvas that experienced gardeners would see as a challenge, but for a complete beginner it must have seemed quite daunting.

But not for long. Over time, Prince Charles assembled a team of advisers, each with a special

BELOW: Prince Charles is a passionate gardener and is not afraid to incorporate modern designs, such as this black and white garden at Highgrove.

area of interest. They included Lady Salisbury for design, plantswoman Rosemary Verey, wild-flower gardening expert Miriam Rothschild and garden historian Sir Roy Strong. By starting close to the house and gradually working out from it, the Prince gradually converted 15 acres to 'proper' gardens.

The first job was to put in some hedges for shelter and privacy. Yew hedges were planted around what was to become the formal rose garden, close to the house. Yew always has a reputation for being painfully slow, but by using massive amounts of manure and sheltering the young plants with a temporary fence of hazel hurdles (always a good tip for establishing a new evergreen hedge), they were soon putting on up to a foot of growth each year.

The walled kitchen garden had to be cleared completely, and it was laid out from scratch in traditional Edwardian country-house style: paths divide the space into four quarters each containing a rose arbour, and a fountain sits in the middle where the paths cross. The planting scheme is anything but Edwardian kitchen garden, though: the walls are covered with roses, and the fruit and vegetables are planted decoratively, potager-style.

Miriam Rothschild was the brains behind the wild-flower lawns leading up to the house. Besides a good mixture of grasses and flowers, she has used yellow rattle, which slows the grass down by parasitizing it. Because the grass is shorter than usual, you can see the wild flowers over the top. The Prince's meadow is cut the old-fashioned way, with a horse-drawn hay cutter, just after the wild flowers have shed their seed, so the colonies increase naturally. In spring, a grass walk is mowed through the meadow leading up to the house, which shows

off the thousands of tulips on either side, all in various shades of mauve, that are planted into the turf in the autumn.

Along one side of the house is the terrace, which is floored with a very country-house pattern of stone slabs and granite sets with plants growing in the gaps. A pair of octagonal 'drystone' pavilions with pointed roofs sit on the terrace.

The woodland garden was made by thinning out an old copse and removing a lot of rickety old trees, then replanting the gaps.

When Highgrove was acquired, the environmental movement was just gathering momentum. As one of the movement's leading advocates, the Prince of Wales put his principles into practice, and now the Prince must be the country's most famous organic gardener. No pesticides, weedkillers or artificial fertilizers are used anywhere on his estate. The ground is improved with compost made by recycling garden rubbish, birds are fed, nest boxes have been put up and piles of rotting logs are left in the woods for beetles and other wildlife. So committed has the Prince become to the organic way of life that there's even a reed-bed sewage treatment plant. At the end of the process what's left is so pure that the pool where it emerges is occasionally visited by kingfishers and dragonflies – always a good indicator of water quality.

The Prince has taken a fair amount of flak over the years for his outspoken views on conservation and organic gardening, but he remains committed to responsible stewardship of the land, and for that he must be admired.

The garden at Highgrove is not open to the public, but the Prince regularly uses it to host events in connection with his public and charitable

THE PRINCE'S CHELSEA

The Prince of Wales has exhibited several gardens at Chelsea Flower Show in recent years.

In 1998 'Impressions of Highgrove' recreated some of the most characteristic elements of his garden at the Chelsea show. It featured a thyme walk and terrace, with a small organic vegetable garden, sponsored by Cartier/*Harpers & Queen*, and designed by Michael Miller of Clifton Nurseries.

In 2001 the 'Carpet Garden', showing elements of Islamic architecture, was again designed by Michael Miller and sponsored by Porcelanosa, from an idea of the Prince's based on the colours and patterns of Middle Eastern carpets at Highgrove.

In 2002 the Prince took the plunge and designed his own 'Healing Garden' in conjunction with Jinny Blom, sponsored by Laurent-Perrier and *Harpers & Queen*. It was an ecologically friendly garden, with a traditionally laid hedge (a first for Chelsea) and a rustic wattle-and-daub shelter made from coppiced timber. The main 'thrust' of the design was three terraces, one planted with edible plants, the second with medicinal plants and the third with poisonous plants. It was dedicated to the memory of his grandmother, Queen Elizabeth the Queen Mother.

Of course, it could be assumed that the Prince has little to do with these gardens, and that others are totally responsible for the designs and choice of materials. But this is not the case, as I discovered when I sat in on a design meeting at Highgrove for the 2002 Chelsea garden. We sat in the Prince's drawing room drinking coffee and eating Duchy Originals biscuits. There were around half a dozen of us – planners and gardeners.

Samples of material were brought in, plans were poured over, and the Prince's approach was most definitely 'hands on'. Would this method of making wattle-and-daub look better than that one? Would a creamier shade of paint be better suited to the final finish? His eye for line is keen (he's a decent amateur painter), and his senses of colour and proportion are well developed.

A pushover? No way. Picky? Yes, but constructively so, and with any luck he'll continue to be involved in the design of gardens for the world's greatest flower show, and keep the monarchy to the fore when it comes to horticultural influence.

OPPOSITE: *Prince Charles with his mother, Queen Elizabeth II, in his 2002 Chelsea garden.*
FAR LEFT: *'Impressions of Highgrove', Chelsea 1998.*
NEAR LEFT: *The Carpet Garden, Chelsea 2001.*
BELOW: *The Healing Garden, Chelsea 2002.*

activities (he is patron or president of about 350 charities), and, through the summer, over 500 groups are also given guided tours of the garden.

The Duchy of Cornwall

When Highgrove was acquired, it came with a 340-acre farm producing arable crops and livestock, which the Prince has added to considerably by buying more land. Three years after moving in the Prince decided to make this the centre of his in-hand farming operations, and it's now known as Home Farm.

Like the garden, the farm is also run on organic lines. Animals are fed on feedstuffs free of genetically modified ingredients and, when need be, livestock are treated with homeopathic remedies. Miles of new hedging have been planted, and

hedges are laid the traditional way. This turns them into living 'woven hurdles', which not only look good but are stock-proof, and growth is so slow that it's usually 20 years or so before they need to be relaid. They look a lot better than 'everyday' countryside hedges that have been slashed to shreds by flail trimmers from the back of a tractor.

The Duchy of Cornwall is a privately owned agricultural estate of over 140,000 acres, roughly half on Dartmoor in Devon and the rest all over the country. Let farms are a major contributor to the Duchy's income.

The Duchy was created in 1337 by Edward III for his son, the Black Prince. The founding charter decreed that the estate should always go to the monarch's eldest surviving son and heir to the throne. Because of the income from the Duchy, unlike other senior members of the Royal Family, Prince Charles is not given an income from the Civil List.

The proceeds from the Duchy have to provide not just the private income for the Duke of Cornwall and his sons, but also the cost of their public duties and charitable activities. Prince Charles, who is the 24th Duke of Cornwall, uses the majority of his income from the Duchy for this latter purpose.

In addition to managing the Duchy of Cornwall in a sustainable way to generate his own income, Prince Charles has also, over the last ten years, put his 'green' principles into practice through Duchy Originals Limited, the company which sells its own range of upmarket organic products and gives all its profits to charity. The range began with biscuits made from organic oats and wheat grown at Home Farm at Highgrove, but it now includes chocolates, preserves, bread, bacon, sausages and soft drinks. Milk comes from the Ayrshire herd at Highgrove, and pigs are reared outdoors on the Duchy estates which also rear turkeys for Christmas. The profits go to the Prince of Wales's Charitable Foundation, over £2.4 million has been passed to the foundation to date. Duchy Original products are available in all major retailers and many independent stores across the country.

The Duchy also owns an oyster farm and a nursery in Cornwall. The nursery, at Lostwithiel, was originally started to supply trees for woodlands on the Duchy estates, but it now specializes in a large range of unusual ornamental shrubs, particularly superior varieties that aren't easily available anywhere else. It's open to the public, and makes a good holiday stopping-off point for anyone in the area.

At Windsor the Queen has a farm shop, which opened in October 2001 in a range of converted Victorian potting sheds on the edge of the Windsor estate. Here are sold products from the various royal farms – milk, cream, yoghurt and ice cream from the royal dairy (as originally established by George III), apples and apple juice from the trees at Sandringham, the Prince of Wales's Duchy Originals and plants from the royal gardens, besides locally produced foods from small specialist suppliers. Coming up to Christmas you'll also find Balmoral Scotch whisky, Windsor farm shop Christmas puddings, and pheasants from the royal estates, some of which will have been shot by members of the royal family. The big novelty for Christmas 2002 was limited edition blue crisps made from rare 'Blue Congo' potatoes.

Royal gardeners have come a long way in a thousand years. No longer do they think dead-heading means executing an opponent in order to pinch his garden. Gone are over-the-top follies and runaway expenditure. Today's royal family is as concerned about cost-effective gardening and caring for the environment as the rest of us, and quite a few of its members are just as likely to get their hands dirty. But whereas royal gardens were once created only for royal use and to impress visiting foreign royalty or nobility, you can now visit most of them, even if they are open only occasionally.

Royal patronage still gives charitable bodies a lot of clout – the Queen is patron of the Royal Horticultural Society and the National Gardens Scheme – and although soap stars are always good pullers, there's still nothing quite so effective as a royal name-tag to add pounds to the sales potential of new plant varieties. Nowadays anyone can have a 'royal' garden – in name at least.

GARDENS TO VISIT

The following list comprises contact details for gardens mentioned in *Royal Gardeners*. All the gardens listed below are open to the public, but as opening times and dates change, please call to confirm before planning your visit.

ANNE HATHAWAY'S COTTAGE
Shottery
Stratford-upon-Avon
Warwickshire CV37 9HH
Tel: 01789 292 100 Fax: 01789 205 014
Email: reception@shakespeare.org.uk
www.shakespeare.org.uk

ARUNDEL CASTLE GARDENS
Arundel
Sussex BN18 9AB
Tel: 01903 882 173 Fax: 01903 884 581
Email: info@arundelcastle.org
www.arundelcastle.org

BALMORAL CASTLE AND GROUNDS
The Estates Office, Balmoral Estates
Ballater
Aberdeenshire AB35 5TB
Tel: 01339 742 534 Fax: 01339 742 034
Email: info@balmoralcastle.com
www.balmoralcastle.com

BIDDULPH GRANGE
Biddulph
Stoke-on-Trent
Staffordshire ST8 7SD
Tel: 01782 517 999 Fax: 01782 510 624
www.nationaltrust.org.uk

BLENHEIM PALACE
Woodstock
Oxfordshire OX20 1PX
Tel: 01993 811 325 Fax: 01993 813 527
Email: administrator@blenheimpalace.com
www.blenheimpalace.com

BRIGHTON PAVILION AND GARDENS
Brighton BN1 1EE
Tel: 01273 290 900
www.royalpavilion.org.uk

BUCKINGHAM PALACE
London SW1A 1AA
Tel: 020 7766 7300 Fax: 020 7766 7321
Email: information@royalcollection.org.uk
www.royal.gov.uk
Ring for opening times of the State Rooms.
Gardens are not open to the public.

CHÂTEAU DE VERSAILLES
78000 Versailles
France
Tel: +33 1 3084 7400
Email: service.multimedia@chateauversailles.fr
www.chateauversailles.fr

CHATSWORTH HOUSE
Chatsworth
Bakewell
Derbyshire DE45 1PP
Tel: 01246 565 300 Fax: 01246 583 536
Email: visit@chatsworth.org
www.chatsworth-house.co.uk

CHELSEA PHYSIC GARDEN
66 Royal Hospital Road
Chelsea
London SW3 4HS
Tel: 020 7352 5646 Fax: 020 7376 3910
Email: maureen@cpgarden.demon.co.uk
www.chelseaphysicgarden.co.uk

COUGHTON COURT
Throckmorton Estates
Alcester
Warwickshire B49 5JA
Tel: 01789 762 435 Fax: 01789 765 544
Email: sales@throckmortons.co.uk
www.coughtoncourt.co.uk

FROGMORE HOUSE AND GARDEN
Gardens and the Royal Mausoleum
Home Park
Windsor
Berkshire SL4 1NJ
Tel: 01753 869 898
E-mail: windsorcastle@royalcollection.org.uk

GLENDURGAN GARDENS
Mawnan Smith
Nr Falmouth
Cornwall TR11 5JZ
Tel: 01326 250 906 Fax: 01872 865 808

HAMPTON COURT PALACE GARDENS
East Molesey
Surrey KT8 9AU
Tel: 0870 752 7777
www.hrp.org.uk

HATFIELD HOUSE
Hatfield
Hertfordshire AL9 5NQ
Tel: 01707 287 010
Email: curator@hatfield-house.co.uk
www.hatfield-house.co.uk

HET LOO PALACE
Koninklijk Park 1
Apeldoorn
Holland
Tel: +31 55 577 2448 Fax: +31 55 521 9983
E-mail: info@paleishetloo.nl
www.paleishetloo.nl

HEVER CASTLE
Hever, Edenbridge
Kent TN8 7NG
Tel: 01732 865 224
www.bbc.co.uk/kent/do_see/castles/hever.shtml

HOLDENBY HOUSE GARDENS
Holdenby House
Holdenby
Northamptonshire NN6 8DJ
Tel: 01604 770 074 Fax: 01604 770 962
Email: enquiries@holdenby.com
www.holdenby.com

KENILWORTH CASTLE
Kenilworth
Warwickshire CV8 1NE
Tel: 01926 852 078 Fax: 01926 851 514
www.coventry.org.uk/heritage2/places/
kenilworthcastle

KENSINGTON PALACE GARDENS
London W8 4PX
Tel: 0870 751 5170
www.hrp.org.uk

LEVENS HALL
Kendal
Cumbria LA8 0PD
Tel: 01539 560 321 Fax: 01539 560 669
Email: email@levenshall.fsnet.co.uk
www.levenshall.co.uk

THE LOST GARDENS OF HELIGAN
Pentewan
St Austell
Cornwall PL26 6EN
Tel: 01726 845 100 Fax: 01726 845 101
Email: info@heligan.com

MONTACUTE HOUSE GARDENS
Montacute
Nr Yeoville
Somerset TA15 6XP
Tel: 01935 823 289 Fax: 01935 826 921
Email: montacute@nationaltrust.org.uk
www.nationaltrust.org.uk

MUSEUM OF GARDEN HISTORY
Lambeth Palace Road
London SE1 7LB
Tel: 020 7401 8865 Fax: 020 7401 8869
Email: info@museumgardenhistory.org
www.cix.co.uk/~museumgh

NASH HOUSE
Chapel Street
Stratford-upon-Avon
Warwickshire CV37 6EP
Tel: 01789 204 016 Fax: 01789 296 083
Email: info@shakespeare.org.uk
www.shakespeare.org.uk

OSBORNE HOUSE AND GARDEN
East Cowes
Isle of Wight PO32 6JY
Tel: 01983 200 022 Fax: 01983 281 380
www.tourist-information-uk.com/
osborne-house.htm

PAINSHILL PARK
Portsmouth Road
Cobham, Surrey KT11 1JE
Tel: 01932 868 113
Email: info@painshill.co.uk
www.painshill.co.uk

PREBENDAL MANOR HOUSE GARDENS
Nassington, Nr Peterborough
Northamptonshire PE8 8QG
Tel: 01780 782 575
Email: info@prebendal-manor.demon.co.uk
www.prebendal-manor.demon.co.uk

QUEEN ELEANOR'S GARDEN
The Great Hall
Winchester, Hampshire SO23 8UL
Tel: 01962 846 476
Email: thegreathall@hants.gov.uk
www.hants.gov.uk/discover/places/eleanor.html

RANGER'S HOUSE AND GARDEN,
GREENWICH PARK
Chesterfield Walk
Greenwich
London SE10
Tel: 020 8853 0035

ROUSHAM HOUSE GARDENS
Steeple Aston
Bicester
Oxfordshire OX25 3QX
Tel: 01869 347 110
www.gardenvisit.com/g/rousham.htm

ROYAL BOTANIC GARDENS KEW
Richmond
Surrey TW9 3AB
Tel: 020 8332 5655 (24 hr) Fax: 020 8332 5197
Email: info@kew.org
www.rbgkew.org.uk

THE ROYAL PARKS
Bushy Park, Green Park, Greenwich Park,
Hyde Park, Kensington Gardens, Regent's Park
(with Primrose Hill), Richmond Park and
St James's Park. *For details see*:
www.royalparks.gov.uk

SANDRINGHAM HOUSE AND GARDENS
The Estate Office
Sandringham
Norfolk PE35 6EN
Estate Office: 01553 772 675
www.sandringhamestate.co.uk

SISSINGHURST
Nr Cranbrook
Kent TN17 2AB
Tel: 01580 710 700 Fax: 01580 710 702

STOURHEAD ESTATE
Stourton
Warminster
Wiltshire BA12 6QD
Tel: 01747 841 152 Fax: 01747 842 005
Email: stourhead@nationaltrust.org.uk
www.nationaltrust.org.uk

STOWE LANDSCAPE GARDENS
Buckingham
Buckinghamshire MK18 5EH
Tel: 01280 822 850 Fax: 01280 822 437
Infoline: 01494 755 568
Email: stowegarden@ntrust.org.uk
www.nationaltrust.org.uk

SYON HOUSE GARDENS
Syon Park
Brentford
Middlesex TW8 8JF
Tel: 020 8560 0881
Email: info@syonpark.co.uk
www.syonpark.co.uk

THEOBALDS PARK
Lieutenant Ellis Way
Cheshunt
Hertfordshire EN7 5HW
Tel: 01992 633 375 Fax: 01992 634 212
www.heritagesites.eu.com/england/theobol.htm

HM TOWER OF LONDON
London EC3N 4AB
Tel: 0870 756 6060
www.hrp.org.uk

WADDESDON MANOR
Waddesdon
Nr Aylesbury
Buckinghamshire HP18 0JH
Tel: 01296 653 203 Fax: 01296 653 212

WESTBURY COURT GARDEN
Westbury-on-Severn
Gloucestershire GL14 1PD
Tel: 01452 760 461 Fax: 01452 760 461
Email: westburycourt@nationaltrust.org.uk
www.nationaltrust.org.uk

WINDSOR CASTLE GARDEN
Windsor
Berkshire SL4 1NJ
Postal Address:
The Official Residences of The Queen,
London SW1A 1AA
Tel: 020 7766 7304 Fax: 020 7930 9625
(Official Residences Information Office)
Email: information@royalcollection.org.uk
www.royal.gov.uk

INDEX

PICTURE CREDITS

BIBLIOGRAPHY

(NOTE: Many of the titles listed below are out of print, and a few are antiquarian books.)

Chelsea: The Greatest Flower Show on Earth, Leslie Geddes-Brown
Cultivated Fruits of Britain, F. A. Roach
The English Garden, Ralph Dutton
Flowers and Flower Lore, Rev. H. Friend
Flowers and Their Histories, Alice M. Coats
Follies, a Guide to Rogue Architecture, Gwyn Headley and Wim
    Meulenkamp
The Formal Garden in England, Reginald Blomfield and F. Inigo Thomas
Gardener's Assistant, Robert Thompson
The Gardener's Labyrinth, Thomas Hill
A Garden of Herbs, Eleanor Sinclair Rohde
Gardens in the Royal Park at Windsor, Lanning Roper
The Garden Triumphant: A Victorian Legacy, David Stuart
Highgrove: Portrait of an Estate, HRH Prince of Wales and Charles Clover
A History of British Gardening, Miles Hadfield
An Illustrated History of Gardening, Anthony Huxley
Medieval Gardens, John Harvey
A Modern Herbal, Mrs Grieve
The New Royal Horticultural Society Encyclopedia of Gardening
The Queen's House: A Social History of Buckingham Palace, Edna Healey
The Royal Gardeners, W. E. Shewell-Cooper
Royal Gardens, Roy Strong
The Story of Gardening, Martin Hoyles
The Story of the Garden, Eleanor Sinclair Rohde
Tulips Portrayed, Sam Segal
The Victorian Kitchen Garden, Jennifer Davies
The Wartime Kitchen and Garden, Jennifer Davies
Windsor Castle: The Official Illustrated History, J. M. Robinson

ACKNOWLEDGEMENTS

Many people have been of tremendous help in the writing of this book and the making of the television series that accompanies it. I am deeply grateful to Her Majesty the Queen for most graciously allowing access to the gardens at Buckingham Palace, Windsor Castle, Sandringham and Balmoral, and to His Royal Highness the Prince of Wales for granting access to the Castle of Mey and for generously showing me the gardens at Highgrove.

So many members of the Royal Household were kindness itself on our visits and made the making of programmes and the writing of this book a great pleasure. Their help has been invaluable and their company hugely enjoyable. Not once did we gain the impression that we were there under sufferance.

Thanks to The Private Estates at Balmoral and Sandringham for help with our filming; The Historic Royal Palaces for filming at Hampton Court Palace and Kensington Palace; to English Heritage for filming at Osborne House; The Crown Estate for filming at Windsor, including Windsor Great Park, Home Park and Savill Garden; The Queen Elizabeth Castle of Mey Trust for filming at the Castle of Mey, and The Royal Parks for filming at Kensington Gardens, Regent's Park and Hyde Park.

We were lucky enough to visit some of the most beautiful houses and gardens in the country. Our thanks to the myriad owners and gardeners who tirelessly gave us access and information, and who weeded borders and clipped acres of box for our arrival at: Basing House, Blenheim Palace, Boscobel House, Burghley House, Biddulph Grange Garden, Carisbrooke Castle, Chatsworth House, Cranborne Manor, Cressing Temple, Ham House, Mizmaze, St Catherine's Hill, Winchester, Hardwick Hall, Het Loo, Holland, Hever Castle, Kenilworth Castle, the Royal Botanic Gardens, Kew, Montacute House, Prebendal Manor, Queen Eleanor's Garden and Winchester Great Hall, Rousham Park, Stowe Landscape Gardens, Thornbury Castle, Vaux le Vicomte, France, Villa d'Este, Villa Lante, Italy, Tudor House, Southampton, Westbury Court Garden, Winchester Cathedral, Wollaton Hall, Yalding Organic Gardens.

In addition, thanks are due to the Royal Horticultural Society for being as helpful as ever at Wisley and the Lindley Library in Vincent Square, London, and to the National Archive for kindly letting us film their treasures.

For research I am hugely indebted to Sue Phillips, Toby Musgrave and Louise Hampden, who have helped me through a thousand years of history. Thanks also go to my watchful editors, Nicky Ross and Helena Caldon, and to Isobel Gillan, who has put together the text and the pictures of this book with great style. Caroline Hughes and Andrew Lawson have taken many of the photographs and have translated gardens that are often difficult to photograph into works of art upon the page.

To my cameramen, Paul Hutchins, Robin Cox, Barrie Foster and Tim Shepherd, sound recordists Gordon Nightingale, Bill Rudolph and Tim Green, and film editors Andi Waite and Chris Mallett, I offer my thanks for making me look and sound human, and to my production team of Anna Gravelle, Louise Hampden, Cassy Walkling, Judy Andrews and Marisa Merry I am indebted, as ever, for their patience and good humour in the face of lapses of memory, tortuous car journeys and foul weather, as well as on the good days and in welcome sunshine.

Dick Colthurst has been as encouraging an executive producer as ever, and Kath Moore a series producer who makes every day's shooting a pleasure thanks to her unbounded enthusiasm, ready laughter, sound judgement and sharp mind.

Finally, my heartfelt thanks to all those royal gardeners past and present who have handed down to us such a generous legacy, and most especially to those who look after the royal gardens today. They are a rare breed and a national treasure. In admiration, this book is dedicated to them.

ALAN TITCHMARSH

This book published to accompany the
BBC Television series *Royal Gardeners*, first broadcast in 2003

Executive Producer: Dick Colthurst

Series Producer: Kath Moore

Published by BBC Worldwide Ltd
Woodlands
80 Wood Lane
London W12 0TT

First published 2003 Reprinted 2003
Text © Copyright Alan Titchmarsh 2003
The moral right of the author has been asserted

BBC Books would like to thank The Royal Botanic Gardens, Kew, and Terry Gough and Susanne Moore at Hampton Court Palace for their help and cooperation with this book.

ISBN: 0 563 48897 2

Commissioning Editor: Nicky Ross
Project Editor: Helena Caldon
Copy Editor: Patricia Burgess
Cover Art Director: Pene Parker
Book Designer: Isobel Gillan
Picture Researcher: Sarah Hopper
Production Controller: Christopher Tinker
Historical Researcher: Toby Musgrave

Set in Scala and Trajan
Printed and bound in Great Britain by
Butler & Tanner Ltd, Frome.
Colour separations by Radstock Reproductions Ltd,
Midsomer Norton.

For more information about this and other BBC books, please visit our website on www.bbcshop.com